FORAGING THE ROCKY MOUNTAINS

Finding, Identifying, and Preparing
Edible Wild Foods in the Rockies

Liz Brown Morgan

FALCONGUIDES

GUILFORD, CONNECTICUT
HELENA, MONTANA

AN IMPRINT OF ROWMAN & LITTLEFIELD

FALCONGUIDES®

Copyright © 2013 by Rowman & Littlefield

ALL RIGHTS RESERVED. No part of this book may be reproduced or transmitted in any form by any means, electronic or mechanical, including photocopying and recording, or by any information storage and retrieval system, except as may be expressly permitted in writing from the publisher.

Falcon, FalconGuides, and Outfit Your Mind are registered trademarks of Rowman & Littlefield.

All photos by Richard Philippe Morgan or Liz Brown Morgan except the following: pp. 1, 11, 152, and 243 licensed by Shutterstock.com; p. 4 by Frank Mayfield, flickr.com; p. 6 by Jerry Kirkhart, flickr.com; p. 7 by Dean Morley, flickr.com.

Map by Melissa Baker © Rowman & Littlefield

Distributed by NATIONAL BOOK NETWORK

Library of Congress Cataloging-in-Publication Data is available on file.

ISBN 978-0-7627-8260-4

Printed in the United States of America

To this ravishingly beautiful thing we call life.
May our careful tending of this hospitable planet allow it to continue on.

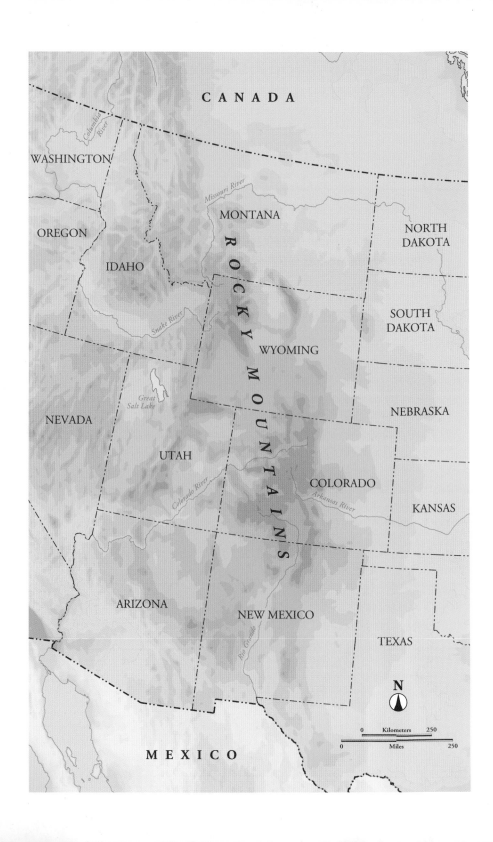

CONTENTS

ACKNOWLEDGMENTS

I am fantastically grateful for the generous assistance of several botanists, wild food specialists, herbalists, photographers and foragers. Learning about wild foods is a lifelong endeavor and my experience and research was supplemented with some incredible and much needed expertise. There is no end to the complexities, the wonders, and the questions that arise as you go deeper into the world of wild edibles, and the people below tackled my endless list of questions.

Rich Morgan, photographs and editing: An enormous thank you to my incredible husband. Rich has joined me on many foraging excursions and photo-taking sessions. He shares my enthusiasm for a wild and nature-oriented lifestyle, and he has been an honest and thoughtful editor and contributor to this book. Rich is a meticulous photographer and biologist and took many of the photographs for this book. He also taught me how to use a camera for the ones I took myself. Rich wrote the section on honeybees. His expertise in bees, photography, and beer brewing, and his background in plant identification, was enormously helpful. Most importantly, Rich reminded me to have fun with this book even as the deadline approached.

Denise C. Wilson: I count myself outrageously fortunate to have worked with Denise on this project. Denise patiently and generously pored over species identification keys to help me confirm the species depicted in the photos for this book. Denise is a professional botanist and has a master's in Integrated Science from the University of Colorado, Denver. She has collected seeds from 350 plant species for seed banking with the National Park Service and Bureau of Land Management's Seeds of Success Program, the Chicago Botanic Garden's Dixon National Tallgrass Prairie Seed Bank, and Kew Gardens' Millennium Seed Bank Program. As an advocate for plant conservation, she has given fifty presentations worldwide from Honolulu to Nairobi. For more about Denise, visit her LinkedIn page: www.linkedin.com/in/denisecwilson.

John Duncan, Oso Negro School: John Duncan is the founder of the Oso Negro School in Taos, New Mexico. He is also an adjunct professor of Wild Food and Wild Medicine at the University of New Mexico, Taos. I sent draft after draft of this book to John, and the insights he came back with were the kinds of things you just can't find in books. John possesses a special depth of knowledge about wild foods, and the assistance he provided was truly extraordinary. If you are in northern New Mexico, you can contact John directly to schedule a nature walk or wildcrafting lesson. For more information visit www.OsoNegroSchool.com.

Katrina Blair, Turtle Lake Refuge: Katrina is the founder of the Turtle Lake Refuge in Durango, Colorado. Katrina and her mighty band of raw, wild foodists bring living the wild food life to extraordinary new heights. Katrina generously shared her wild food wisdom with me and helped answer some of the most difficult questions I had when trying to finalize this book. If you are in the Durango area, stop by to get inspired and pick up some wild snacks for the road. Katrina's cookbook, *Local Wild Life: Turtle Lake Refuge's Recipes for Living Deep,* demonstrates her mastery of wild cuisine and is a must for any forager's bookshelf. Find more info at www.TurtleLakeRefuge.org.

Others also provided valuable assistance. Thanks to Marisa Heidt for helping me with the tree section. Marisa is an environmental educator and has worked for the City of Boulder as an urban forestry assistant and for the Boulder County arborist. Thanks also to Briggs Wallis, an herbalist, nutritionist, and natural health practitioner in Boulder, Colorado, for careful editing of plant uses. Jared Urchek (www.BoulderMushrooms.com) provided fascinating insight into wild mushrooms. Although we ended not including any mushrooms in the book, discussing mushrooms with Jared is always amazing. My thanks also goes to Julie Hayes for her thoughtful insights and editing assistance. And thanks to Andy Fischer (www.SacredEarthDesign.com) for taking the time to discuss wild foods in the context of permaculture.

INTRODUCTION

The historical significance of wild edibles cannot be overstated. For the vast majority of human existence, including the present time, humans have been foragers. Humans and civilizations across the planet, from the very beginning, have persisted and achieved greatness because of the edible nourishment that the earth naturally provides. Even now, almost everyone I meet has some sort of foraging story: a warm yarrow poultice used to treat a rope burn; a crazy aunt with a dandelion salad fixation; reliance on old family herbal recipes; tasting honeysuckle from mom's midwestern garden. Our family stories, our personal histories, are intrinsically tied to the things the earth provides for us. The fruits of the earth are the abundance upon which health, security, and happiness arise. I am so pleased to be part of the resurgence of the foraging mindset, and I hope this book helps readers connect even more deeply with this beautiful, hospitable, life-nourishing planet.

On my personal journey from the grocery into the woods, as I have begun to learn the vastness of the wild edible world, my connection to the pulse of life on earth has greatly deepened. My connection to health and ecosystems and global rejuvenation is now easier to identify and comprehend. It's like awakening into knowledge that I was yearning for from early on in my life. Without this understanding, my place in the world was confusing. With it, I recognize that I am part of this place, I belong to it, and it nourishes me on every level. I can see and understand that we are interconnected in a real way to the plants, and that gives me not only bodily health but also a higher level of inner peace.

My hope in writing this book is that people will learn not to poison the edible plants that they call weeds and start tending their gardens, landscapes, and wildernesses in ways that allow them to harvest, eat, and thoroughly enjoy the edible history of the planet and of humankind. I believe that the truest calling of our species is to tend the life of planet earth with love and compassion. That means caring for humans, animals, plants, bugs and entire ecosystems. This is one step in the process of improving our relationship with the earth, rejuvenating natural systems, creating global sustainability, and setting a foundation for our own health and happiness—and for our civilization to attain new heights.

Go outside and eat a dandelion. It really is that easy.

Scope of the Book

This book is mostly focused on edible wild plants along with other recreational and safe uses, such as crafts, bathing, rituals, smudges, and aromatherapy. The book describes edible herbs, shrubs, berries, and trees.

I often mention medicinal uses; however, this **is not an herbal medicine book.** I mention medicinal uses only to give the reader additional background on the wide array of uses for each plant. Use these mentions as a starting point only for further research to deepen your understanding of wild plants. This should not be taken as medicinal advice in any way, and it is a good idea to consult with a professional herbalist before using any wild plant medicinally.

I have also included at least one recipe for each edible plant. The focus is on fresh foods prepared simply. Most recipes include only one wild food, so you don't have to worry about difficult-to-find ingredients. Look up a recipe for the plants you have foraged; the rest of the ingredients will be basic household staples.

My goal in the description, comments, and recipe sections is to provide a foundational understanding about how to use each plant. Simple discussions about edibility, harvesting, preparation, and complementary food pairings will help you get started on your journey to creating delicious wild meals. Recipes range from raw to cooked, vegan to animal products, and dairy and gluten free. I also tried to think about what time of year different wild foods are available and create recipes that make sense given what else is in season.

There are many beverage recipes in this book, mostly teas. Wild edibles in drink form can be a great way to take in a variety of nutrients, try different wild plants, and tempt our taste buds. Compared with other cultures that utilize hundreds of plants in drinks and healing teas, our culture has less variety. We drink so much soda, artificial fruit punch, alcohol, artificially colored and sugary energy drinks, and caffeine that drinking has become a depleting activity. We have to spend time, energy, and nutrients recovering from the things we drink. The teas in this guide will fortify rather than deplete. I recommend making teas out of as many wild plants as possible. It is a fun way to engage with wild edibles.

This book also provides detailed plant descriptions that are clear for a layperson with little or no plant identification experience. I have attempted to include key pieces of information needed to set a particular plant apart from similar looking ones.

Warnings and Safety

Since there are many poisonous plants in the wild, and many look similar to edible plants, beginning foragers should spend their time looking at and identifying plant species but not eating them. If you do not know for sure that a plant is safe to eat, you should assume it is poisonous.

Not all poisonous plants are listed in this book. Just because you don't see a certain plant listed as poisonous **does not mean it is safe** to consume. You must be sure that you have identified a plant correctly before you eat it. This often is not possible no matter your foraging experience level. There are deadly plants that can be encountered anywhere. Others may not cause death but can cause moderate to severe illness or lasting damage to your body. I cannot underscore the importance of this warning enough. Consult many sources—books, photos from a variety of websites, and professional herbalists and botanists. Go on herb walks with experts to confirm your identifications. Until you feel you are expert at your identification skills, don't make the mistake many others have made and end up poisoning yourself.

Always remember that there is a lot you don't know. Your job as a forager is to learn when exact matters, and when it doesn't, and how exact you need to be.

Pay attention to the specific uses listed. Not all parts of all plants can be eaten, and not all parts can be eaten raw.

Always be aware of the potential for allergic reactions to wild plants. After you have positively identified a plant, and you have ruled out the potential for poisonous lookalikes, do an allergy test on yourself. Rub a small amount on your skin. If you get a reaction, do not consume this species. Next, if you have not reacted, prepare appropriately and take a tiny nibble and see what happens. If you have no negative reaction after a couple of hours, take a larger bite. Then progress slowly toward eating a normal amount of the plant. Keep in mind that the potency of wild plants varies with location, growing conditions, and subspecies, so just because something worked for you one day does not mean the same amount will be OK to consume on another day.

Please note: This advice is for healthy adults only. In addition, pregnant women should not generally eat any wild plants without consulting a professional. If you are not a healthy adult, are a child or elderly, have any sort of illness, are taking medication, are pregnant or breastfeeding, or your health is compromised in any way, you should only try new wild foods and medicines under strict supervision of a very good herbalist. Wild plants are potent and often good for you, but you need to maintain a high level of care when trying new ones.

Always pay close attention to your own and your friends' reactions to wild foods. In some cases anaphylaxis can result. Anaphylaxis is a very serious condition that results in the closing of the airways, hives, asthma-like symptoms, a swelling in the throat, and difficulty swallowing and breathing. It can result in death if not treated right away. If you or anyone you are with begins to experience difficulty breathing or any of these symptoms, seek medical attention immediately.

The basic rule of thumb when foraging is: Don't eat anything or rub it on your skin unless you are 100 percent sure you know what it is. The vast majority of plants will not kill you; however, a few, such as poison hemlock, certainly can. Don't take this stuff lightly. And by all means, do not ruin a lovely day of foraging by making a fatal or near-fatal mistake.

Unknown allergies or incorrect identification are always a possibility, and when you're in the backcountry, rescue may not come in time. Remoteness is wonderful, but you have to maintain focus on keeping you and your crew safe. It is best not to try wild edibles for your first time in the wild. Harvest them, take them home, and try small amounts in controlled settings where you have access to medical attention if needed.

Plan on spending months or even years learning about plants before you consider eating them. One stupid mistake, one tiny taste, can spell disaster. My husband and I have a rule: We don't taste new wild foods alone. Our decision came after one occasion where I was alone and decided to eat a wild plant that I had not eaten before. I was certain I had identified the plant correctly; I had done thorough research and was sure the plant was safe to eat if prepared correctly. After ingestion I became anxious and began to panic. I had nobody to consult with or to discuss my situation with. I began to fear I had possibly poisoned myself. Once I started panicking, I was unable to monitor my symptoms properly, since my mental state was causing me to have an increased heart rate and other strange sensations that seemed like symptoms. I drove myself to the emergency room, where I eventually was told I was fine. There's nothing like a $1,200 medical bill and the belief that you made a huge mistake to make you set up some personal protocols. Lesson learned, and luckily I was not actually poisoned.

Check Local Regulations

You cannot forage everywhere. Before harvesting on any public lands, check the rules and regulations. Different types of government-owned land have different rules about foraging. In some places it is strictly prohibited; on others it is perfectly acceptable. If you want to harvest on private lands, you will obviously need the landowner's permission.

You should also be aware that along our roads and highways, the Colorado Department of Transportation (CDOT—it may be another agency in your state) routinely sprays herbicides and poisons plants that they consider to be noxious weeds. Some of these so called "noxious weeds" are actually edible wild species, or live very close to edible species. Some are covered in this book. One example is great mullein. CDOT personnel do not leave signs warning of the spraying except while they are actually spraying, so you have to call the state or county to find out what areas are safe and which have been sprayed.

I'd like to see teams of foragers work with state officials to harvest these plants. Let's see wild harvest parties replace poison trucks!

Oxalates

Oxalates are compounds that occur naturally in many plants and foods, including spinach, lamb's-quarter, dock, peanuts, almonds, pecans, beans, chocolate, plums, currants, figs, soy, swiss chard, parsley, black pepper, okra, sweet pota-toes, beer, amaranth, and purslane. Studies have linked oxalates to a variety of illnesses, including kidney stones, fibromyalgia, autism, thyroid disease, vuv-lodynia, chronic obstructive pulmonary disease (COPD), cystic fibrosis, asthma, pain disorders, and chronic fatigue syndrome. The question is whether eating foods high in oxalates actually causes these problems. The studies I have found indicate that while eating oxalates can worsen these illnesses, there is usually some other underlying cause for the disease itself.

Oxalic acid occurs naturally in our bodies. The amount of oxalic acid in our bloodstream is not necessarily directly related to the amount we eat. Certain fac-tors, such as taking antibiotics, candida (yeast) outbreaks, or fungal infections, can have a much more significant relation to our oxalate levels.

When levels become too high, serious problems can occur. For people with the diseases listed above, a reduced oxalate diet appears to be a helpful part of treatment. That does not mean that eating normal amounts of oxalates will trig-ger these diseases in healthy people.

For healthy people who do not have an oxalate-related problem, most foods rich in oxalates are considered healthy. In other words, don't eat pounds and pounds of oxalate-rich foods and nothing else. Such large quantities can be det-rimental, in some cases even fatal. Make these foods part of a diverse diet.

Where to Begin

For beginners, it can be overwhelming to figure out where to start. To help, I've created a list for first-time foragers. It includes some of my favorite wild edibles that are easy to find and identify, plentiful, and fun to eat.

Beginner's Foraging List:
- **Dandelion** (early spring). One of the first plants to bloom provides greens and a great way to start the foraging season. Leave some flowers for the bugs.
- **Lamb's-quarter** (greens in early spring to summer). Wild spinach; an abso-lute necessity in the kitchen.
- **Sheep sorrel** (summer). A bit difficult to distinguish from dock and other similar looking plants at first. The whale-shaped leaves and their unmistak-able tangy flavor make making a positive ID relatively easy.
- **Fireweed** (mid to late summer). Big, beautiful, delicately tasty flowers can be eaten raw.
- **Sunflower** (late summer). Enjoy the small, nutritious seeds.
- **Thimbleberry** (late summer). Bigger, juicier, sweeter than a raspberry.
- **Chokecherry** (late summer). Big juicy droops hanging from thin branches. Found prolifically throughout the region.

- **Plums** (late summer). If I could, I would have a bowl of wild plums with me at all times.
- **Western blue flax** (late summer to fall). A relative of commercial flax seeds, the seeds are smaller but well worth it. Fields bloom light purple in early summer.
- **Apples** (late summer to fall). American settlers planned for a sustainable and delicious food future by planting apples trees across the West. Their legacy remains.
- **Juniper berries** (year-round). I nibble on the young green and the old dark ones. Eat one or two along the trail for a mouth freshener, as an antiseptic, and to take your mind off the miles.

Some very basic supplies are helpful when you go foraging. Bring a plant identification book, or a few books. It's helpful to use books when conducting your plant identifications while out in the field. There are characteristics that you might forget or not notice if you wait until you get home. It's not always possible to identify a plant in the field. In that case, take samples and photos if you wish, and resume identification at home with additional research materials.

Bring a pair of scissors to clip off leaves or small branches. Also bring containers. Many people use plastic bags, but I prefer to use sturdy, reusable containers. Bring a variety of sizes, depending on what you are going to harvest. Bring some way to label the containers. You can write directly on them or use tape and a permanent marker. Also bring a pen and paper to take notes and write down questions. If you are digging roots or tubers, you will want a trowel or shovel. Heavy gardening clippers may be appropriate depending on what you plan to harvest.

A camera is another extremely valuable tool. If you have questions about a plant's identification, you can take lots of photos and then go over the details at home. From personal experience, I recommend a brightly colored camera—if you lose it in some tall grass, it will be a little easier to find.

Where to Find Wild Edibles: Range and Habitats

Wild edibles are absolutely everywhere. They grow on the highest mountain peaks and poke out of little cracks in sidewalks in the depths of the biggest cities. Once you start looking, you will see them everywhere: along creeks and ditches and rivers and growing out of canyon walls. Most plants are edible in one way or another.

You have probably walked over common plantain and red clover. You have probably sped by ripe chokecherries and wild plums comfortably lodged in an old canyon ditch. Even many grasses are edible. Every farm in the world has abundant weeds. Almost all of these are wild edibles. Along every highway and road and trail, you will find wild edibles. If you have a garden, you can find wild edibles there too.

Wild edibles can be native or endemic (existed in the United States before Europeans arrived) or introduced (brought here in the years since Europeans arrived on this continent). Introduced plants are also called nonnatives. Many nonnatives have become perfectly acceptable, integrated members of our local ecosystems. However, when nonnatives find themselves in habitats that are particularly well suited for them, they can become extremely aggressive and outcompete native plants, causing imbalance and often serious problems in the system. When this happens nonnatives are considered invasive nuisance species. Eradication attempts often ensue. Oftentimes the line between nonnative and invasive is not terribly well defined, and poisonous eradication efforts can do more harm than good.

Habitat Ranges Defined

The Rocky Mountain region is filled with diverse microclimates. What grows at 5,500' in elevation can be much different than what grows at 9,000' . What grows on the north (colder, darker, moister) side of a hill is usually different than what grows on the south (warmer, sunnier, drier) side. What grows in a valley is different than what grows on the adjoining hillside. What grows under a tree is different than what grows in a ditch or at the base of a warm rock cliff. Temperature variations are dramatic in these different zones and create very particular microclimates.

Because of these microclimates, it is difficult to give exact times of year when certain plants will sprout, flower, go to seed, etc. In parts of the country where the terrain is more uniform, growth cycles are more uniform across the region. In our region spring comes at least a month earlier in Boulder, Colorado, than it does around my home in the foothills, 3,000' higher. Elevation is a huge factor, even though distance in miles can be quite short. Likewise, plant size and productivity vary dramatically with elevation and microclimate. The higher you go, the smaller the plants generally are. Plant height and leaf size are smaller. Fruit production might be less.

Because of this, when trying to give information about time of year to expect certain things from certain plants (when to harvest fruit, when to harvest young leaves) I have used terms like "early-spring" rather than "June," because while June might be early spring at 9,000', it is late spring at lower elevations. Also, seasonal variations in weather patterns, especially temperature and moisture, have a huge impact on when plants do what. Drought can cause plants to go to seed months earlier than they would in a wet year, when they grow relatively stress free. The information I have provided should be used as guidelines, but it is up to you to assess the season and learn how plants respond in your particular microclimate.

The US Department of Agriculture (USDA) has an exceptional online resource for determining whether a plant grows in your area (http://plants.usda .gov). The USDA plant database provides locator maps that drill down to the county level, so you can see if a particular species has been located in a particular county. Plants migrate, and these maps are not always up to date, but they are a pretty good resource.

Zones used in this book:

Alpine zone: Also called the Alpine tundra, this is the highest elevation. It is above tree line, which varies depending on region. This biotic zone has a very short growing season, about six to eight weeks. Many species of hardy plants grow here, though they all remain small as a result of ripping winds and cold temperatures. Throughout most of the US Rockies, this zone starts at an altitude of about 12,000' elevation. In the Yukon, the northern reaches of the Rocky Mountains, it can be as low as about 2,500' in elevation.

Subalpine zone: Mid- to high-range mountain elevation zone from about 9,000' or 10,000' in elevation to about 11,500' or 12,000'. Marked by Engelmann spruce, bristlecone pine, aspen, subalpine fir, and, toward the high part of this zone, a variety of trees stunted by the severe conditions called krummholz. Also open meadows filled with yellow glacier lily, lupine, shooting star, and columbine.

Montane zone: Mid to lower range mountainous elevations. Usually from about 8,000' to 10,000' in elevation. Ponderosa pine, juniper, Douglas fir and Gambel oak.

Foothills: Ranges from about 4,900' to 8,000' in elevation. Species include juniper, sagebrush, piñon pine, and larkspur.

Riparian areas: Can exist in any elevation zone. Includes areas directly along water, such as creeks, rivers, flood zones, and wetlands.

How Much to Pick: Sustainable Harvesting Guidelines

Nature impacts us everyday, whether we know it or not, and we impact it. Our impacts on nature extend far beyond just what we do when we are out in the woods. The actions we take in our daily lives also significantly impact nature.

The Leave No Trace philosophy (take only pictures, leave only footprints) is an excellent moral code of conduct for backpacking trips, but it can't extend to foraging—or to life in general. Everything we do has an impact. It is our choice to decide how big that impact is going to be and whether it will be negative or positive, loving, or careless. Foraging is one piece of a thoughtful human lifestyle that keeps nature in mind at all times with the goal of positive, rejuvenating, sustainable impacts on natural systems. The point is that harvesting wild foods ultimately might have more of a positive impact on the world than buying factory-farmed, overly packaged foods. If we look at foraging as a systemic transformation, certainly it can be done in ways that may leave a trace, but are far more positive than current methods of obtaining sustenance.

Foraging should be seen as an exercise in tending. Foraging is a relationship with the earth that does not need to be harmful. The earth is abundantly filled with food, and if we treat her appropriately, that abundance continues just as it has for thousands of generations. It is important to learn to forage (and live our lives) in ways that makes us good stewards of the land. Foragers need to understand how to harvest thoughtfully. The goal is to enjoy food now and also to ensure food for next year, the year after, and forever.

If you see just one apple tree filled with apples, the foraging strategy is different than if you see just one wild onion. You can take lots of apples (leaving some for wild animals, some to rot on the ground, and some for other people), but you should definitely leave the onion untouched until you find a big robust stand of it. Foraging habits depend on the type of plant or fruit and its abundance.

For example, if I harvest a bowl full of yarrow leaves in mid-October, just before the first frost, I am not harming the plant. It has already flowered and is on its way to winter dormancy. If, however, I harvest all the yarrow leaves from a stand in June, before the yarrow has flowered, it could be seriously detrimental. It could prevent the plant from flowering, providing food to pollinators and setting seed. Timing and species matter.

Another example: Nodding thistle is a biennial, so future germination of the species is reliant on seed production. If I take all the fluffy seeds from a stand of nodding thistle to stuff a pillow, that will have a negative consequence on next year's germination potential. Creeping thistle, on the other hand, is a perennial. It spreads mostly through root systems. Its seeds germinate but not prolifically, and the species relies more on its perennial root systems. It wouldn't be as harmful to harvest the creeping thistle seeds. Of course I'd also have to think about who eats the thistle seeds and what impact my harvest will have on those wild creatures.

Every species' individual traits must be carefully considered when making decisions about what, when, and how much to harvest. In each plant chapter I have included information about whether it is annual, biennial, or perennial. But keep in mind too that if it's a drought year and animals have trouble finding food, it may be the right decision to harvest far less than you would in a more abundant year. How much to take, ultimately, has more to do with how much you know and how well you can assess the situation than it has to do with adherence to strict rules. We humans have the ability to destroy ecosystems, and foragers should keep that in mind.

Samuel Thayer explains that our culture's relationship with nature is either too destructive (we take too much and disregard greater ecosystem needs) or we put it on a pedestal and don't interact with it at all. Thayer says, "We destroy it for profit, or we idealize its beauty and preserve it untouched" (*Nature's Garden: A Guide to Identifying, Harvesting, and Preparing Edible Wild Plants*).

Conversely, the intimate, interactive relationship between forager and nature is what creates the understanding about how to properly manage, rejuvenate, and protect natural systems. We can have living, workable, sustainable places where we can take in the beauty and also benefit by foraging in that place. It is not all or nothing. We know that a mutually beneficial relationship between forager and nature is possible, because our ancestors on this continent and across the world learned to tend wild nature in ways that created ongoing abundance. That is the goal.

Sustainable Harvesting Guidelines: How Much to Pick Depending on Species Density

This table is a guideline only. It is a very rough estimate of how much might be appropriate to harvest in certain situations. Always use your senses, assess the situation, and harvest less than you think you should.

Number of individuals of species in area	How much OK to pick
Less than 20	None. Observe only. Harvesting may be acceptable for purposeful weed mitigation for a farm, park, roadway, or garden.
Between 20 and 50	May be acceptable to harvest some leaves or fruits. Depends on time of year, ecosystem needs, and species. For very aggressive species (like creeping thistle) or weeds that readily reseed (dandelion or evening primrose), it may be acceptable to harvest more aggressively. Consider pollinator needs.
About 50	May be acceptable to harvest a few plants, flowers, roots. Consider whether harvest kills the whole plant. Depends on time of year, ecosystem needs, and species. Leave the biggest and strongest to reproduce.
About 100	May be acceptable to harvest 5–10 percent. Consider time of year, ecosystem needs, and species. May be acceptable to harvest all parts of plant. Leave the biggest and strongest to reproduce.
An acre or more filled with the species	May be acceptable to harvest 5–10 percent. Confirm that species is abundant. May be acceptable to harvest all parts of plant. Leave the biggest and strongest to reproduce.

The best way to understand how much to take is to monitor the ecosystems from year to year. Go back the following year and see how the ecosystem is doing post harvest. It is an ongoing learning process.

If we forage thoughtfully and with the goal of ensuring future harvests, we can consciously participate in a long-lasting relationship between humans and plants, humankind and nature. If done right it is bountiful, mutually life giving, and a whole lot of fun.

How to Identify Plants

The most important thing about identifying plants for the purpose of eating them is to be absolutely sure that you have identified the correct plant. The Convention on Biological Diversity (www.cbd.int) says there are about 400,000 species of flowering plants worldwide, about 15,000 species of ferns, 1,000 gymnosperms (conifers), and 23,000 mosses. For comparison, the CBD says there are about one million species of insects, 28,000 species of fish, 10,000 species of birds, and 5,400 species of mammals (www.guardian.co.uk/science/2010/sep/19/scientists-prune-world-plant-list).

It is important to understand that the plant species listed in this book are just a tiny sampling of all plants that you will find when foraging. It is very easy to think you have found something but get it wrong. There are just so many species and varieties out there. Most importantly, **do not make it fit.** If a plant does not exactly match the description, it is likely not the right plant.

The scent and texture of a plant are often telling. If a species is described as being very pungent, smell it to see if your senses can recognize the smell described. The bark of ponderosa pine has a strong vanilla smell. If you smell a tree and smell nothing, it is probably a different species. If a stalk is supposed to be ridged, feel it, and observe it to be sure.

I recommend bringing plant ID books out in the field with you and making your identifications, as much as possible, while in the field. Take pictures, and then confirm with more sources when back at home. There are things you will miss or forget if you wait until you are home.

Leaf Identification

Though less sexy than flowers and fruits, leaves are an important feature in identifying a species. Fruits and flowers are often shorter lived, so you are frequently left with only the leaves to evaluate. Key leaf factors include:

Leaf shape (oval, palmate, linear, heart shaped, etc.)
Leaf size (tiny, small, large, etc.)
Leaf arrangement (alternate, opposite, basal, whorled)
Leaf location (along the ground or up the stalk)
Leaf color and texture (darker on top, waxy, fuzzy, etc.)

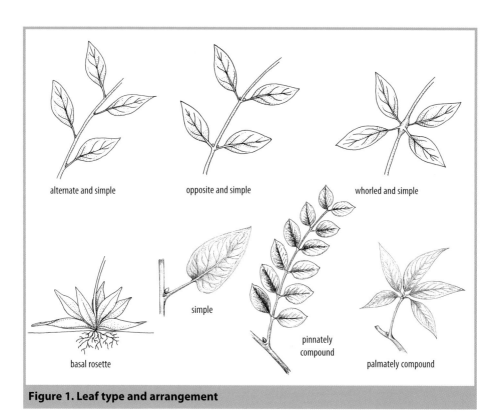

alternate and simple

opposite and simple

whorled and simple

basal rosette

simple

pinnately compound

palmately compound

Figure 1. Leaf type and arrangement

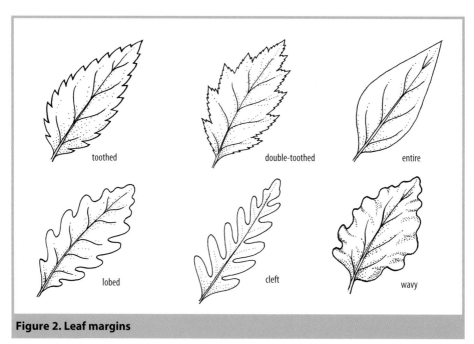

toothed

double-toothed

entire

lobed

cleft

wavy

Figure 2. Leaf margins

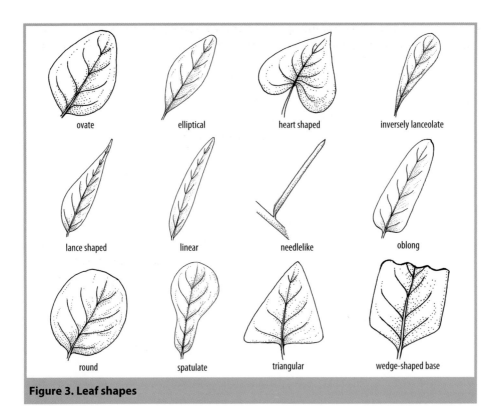

ovate	elliptical	heart shaped	inversely lanceolate
lance shaped	linear	needlelike	oblong
round	spatulate	triangular	wedge-shaped base

Figure 3. Leaf shapes

Basic Terms

Alternate: Leaves or leaflets arranged along the leaf stem in a staggered, not opposite, pattern.

Basal florette: A leaf cluster arising from the base of the plant. Often circular and arising in the first year for a biennial. The stalk will emerge from the basal florette in the second year.

Compound: Leaf formation where the leaf is divided into separate leaflets. The leaf blade is not continuous. Opposite of simple leaf structure. Leaflets often look like individual leaves.

Decumbent: Growth pattern indicating the plant is low lying or grows along the ground.

Entire: Used to describe leaf margins or leaf edges that are continuous and smooth, not toothed or lobed.

Lanceolate or lance-shaped: Leaf shape that is longer than it is wide and wider in the middle than at the ends. Usually wider portion is somewhat below the middle, tapering to a point at the leaf tip.

Linear: Leaf shape that is long and very narrow, with sides that are about parallel.

Lobed: Deep, rounded indents along the leaf edges. Can occur on any shaped leaf.

Margin: Leaf edge.

Palmate: Lobes or leaflets radiate out from a central point, usually from the top of the petiole, or leaf stem. Generally forming a somewhat circular pattern.

Pinnate: A compound leaf consisting of multiple leaflets arranged along a common axis or leaf stem. Generally forming a somewhat straight lined pattern as opposed to palmate leaves.

Rosette: A circular cluster of leaves at the base of a plant; the basal rosette.

Serrate: Leaf margins or edges that are not smooth but toothed or jagged. Can be pointed or rounded, deeply toothed or shallowly toothed.

Simple: A leaf that has just one part; not divided into leaflets.

Trifoliate: Clusters of three leaves or three leaflets, like a clover.

Whorl: A circular formation of three or more leaves or other structures radiating out creating a circle or spiral around the stalk.

Fruit and Flower Identification

You will also want to inspect a plant's flowers and fruits, depending on the season. Color, shape, and how they are positioned on the stalk are important. Look at whether flowers form in a pointed or rounded cluster or as an umbel, whether they are showy or discreet. Look at petal size, number and arrangement.

Basic Terms

Bract: A type of leaf that embraces or cups a flower or an inflorescence.

Bud: A developing, unopened flower.

Disc floret (disc flower): Small flowers in the center of a composite flower head. Lacks petals.

Floret: A small flower, typically one in a cluster making up a composite flower head. Can be ray or disc.

Inflorescence: The flowering parts of a plant; sometimes a single flower, sometimes a cluster.

Ray floret (ray flower): Small flower resembling one petal.

Umbel: An umbrella-shaped inflorescence.

Umbellet: A smaller umbrella-shaped flower cluster that together with other umbellets make up the umbel.

Life Cycle, Root, Stem, and Special Features Identification

Also pay attention to location and habitat. You can use the range descriptions in this book for general locations.

If a species is said to live only in moist soil and you believe you have found it on a dry sand dune, this discrepancy should be taken into consideration. Could it have been appropriately moist when the plant germinated? Or perhaps it is not the plant you think it is.

Often there will be one tiny bit of information needed to separate a particular species from another; for example, an almost unnoticeable strip of hair growing along the stalk or an obvious bloom (white coating) on the stalk.

Also look at the overall appearance of a plant. Does it grow along the ground, as a shrub or a tree? Height, width, and shape are important factors. Stem, roots, and special features should also be carefully reviewed.

Basic Terms

Biennial: A plant that lives for two years, often putting out leaves in year one and flowers, fruits, and seeds in the second year. Not perennial or annual.

Bloom: A white powdery coating on a stalk or leaf.

Herbaceous: Fleshy plant, not woody; why we call herbs herbs.

Rhizome: An underground stem or root that spreads and produces new plants. Common reproduction method for perennials.

Stem: The main stalk, usually growing upward.

Taproot: Type of root that is thick and often extends deep into the earth, like a carrot.

Woolly: Having fine, soft, felt- or wool-like hairs covering the stalk or leaves of a plant. Often giving a whitish or silvery hue.

Plant Names

Plant names are useful in identification and in understanding the uses and other characteristics of plants. I have included a lot of common names for each plant where they exist, because they are often very telling. For example, Satan's bolete is a poisonous lookalike to the king bolete. It's called "Satan" because it will make you very sick. Great mullein is also called lungwort because it is used medicinally to treat lung problems. Mallow is called cheeseweed because its tender, edible seeds look just like a wheel of cheese. Yarrow is called soldier's woundwort because it can be used to stop bleeding. Fleabane repels fleas. The point is that names can also be useful in plant identification and in gaining a deeper understanding about the history and uses of the species.

The Latin names listed are the currently accepted genus and species. Genus is listed first; species, second. In some cases it is important (because of inedible lookalikes or other confusion points) to identify the plant down to the species level. For others, like wild roses, it is not.

Start Foraging (by Rich Morgan, Photographer)

Foraging should be a fun and relaxing experience. Don't worry about eating plants at first if you are a beginner. Just step out your back door and into your backyard or take a hike somewhere wild, and start to look at the plants. Identify them, recognize them, photograph them, and have fun. Once you have some practice and are confident with your identification skills of several species, then maybe start to forage and start to eat the bounties the earth has to offer. But don't let any of the warnings discourage you from beginning the journey. To practice, look, smell, and photograph is harmless and is how everyone begins. So get out there and get started. Hope to see you out on the trails.

Poisonous Plants

WARNING: Do not ingest any of the species in this chapter, as they are highly poisonous.

WESTERN POISON IVY
Toxicodendron rydbergii

Family: Anacardiaceae

Other names: Green western poison ivy, poison ivy, *Rhus rydbergii*

WARNING: Allergic contact dermatitis can occur when the skin comes in contact with poison ivy. This plant contains urushiol (as do poison sumac and poison oak), an oil that can cause a severe allergic reaction. Symptoms include hives, rash, swelling, itching, and pain. Redness, bumps, and large puss-filled blisters can also result.

For highly sensitive people, anaphylaxis can result. Anaphylaxis is very serious and results in the closing of the airways, often with a swelling in the throat, and can result in death. If you or anyone in your party begins to experience difficulty breathing or the throat starts to close, he or she should be taken to the hospital **immediately.**

Description

Western poison ivy is a low-growing rhizomatous perennial growing up to 4' tall. Leaves are alternate and compound, each consisting of three large, rounded leaflets. Leaflets are 1"–6" long and 1"–4" wide. They are usually shiny but otherwise can vary from fairly smooth to toothed to slightly lobed. Leaves turn from reddish when young to glossy green in summer. In fall they turn red, orange, or yellow.

Five-petaled, nondescript, cream or light greenish flower clusters along the leaf axils give way to white berries, or drupes. Each drupe is less than ½" in diameter and contains one seed.

Poison ivy often forms a dense ground cover and can span several square feet or even an acre.

Range and Habitat

Fertile, moist soil of all types from British Columbia throughout the United States except the southeastern states. From sea level up to 8,500' in elevation. Found along roadsides, on sand dunes, in forests and along forest edges, especially near creeks, ditches, and areas where floods sometimes occur.

Comments

The old saying about poison ivy, "Leaflet three, let it be," is a good reminder not to touch this three-leaved plant. Related to eastern poison ivy (*Toxicodendron radicans*), which is very similar but is vine-like and climbs high into trees. Western poison ivy does not climb.

A salve or remedy against poison ivy can be made with gumweed (*Grindelia squarrosa*).

Take a lesson from my friend the coach, who washed clothes that had come into contact with poison ivy with a load of uncontaminated laundry. The toxic oil spread to everything. Every time he got dressed, the painful rash would reappear. Wearing his hat caused his eyes to swell shut, and he finally realized it was time for a new wardrobe.

WATER HEMLOCK
Cicuta maculata

Family: Apiaceae
Other names: Spotted water hemlock, spotted cowbane, common water hemlock, poison parsnip, spotted parsley
Lookalikes: All the white umbelled species, including water parsnip (*Sium suave*), osha (*Ligusticum porteri*), angelica (*Angelica grayi*), Queen Anne's lace (*Daucus carota*), wild parsleys (*Lomatium* spp.), and poison hemlock (*Conium maculatum*; also poisonous)
WARNING: Extremely poisonous. Do not ingest. If you touch it, wash hands immediately. It's probably a good idea not to smell it either.

Description
This native biennial or perennial is similar to poison hemlock, but the leaves are coarser. Leaves are arranged in pinnate clusters of three (sometimes one to two). Leaflets are sharply toothed along the leaf edges and linear or lance-shaped with a pointed tip. Leaflets are up to about 4" long with a central vein and radial veins. The radial veins terminate in the notches of the leaflet teeth, not at the tips.

The root is hairless. The stalk is sometimes branched and reaches 3'–6' tall. It can have purple markings, but not always.

Range and Habitat
Found from Alaska to Texas in moist to wet soil. Grows in high altitudes like osha does.

Comments
I have been told this is the most poisonous plant on the continent.

POISON HEMLOCK
Conium maculatum

Family: Apiaceae

Other names: Hemlock, devil's bread, cigue maculee, cigue tachetee, deadly hemlock, poison parsley

Lookalikes: All the white umbelled species, especially osha (*Ligusticum porteri*). Also looks like osha del campo, or angelica (*Angelica grayi*), Queen Anne's lace (*Daucus carota*), wild parsleys (*Lomatium* spp.), water parsnip (*Sium suave*), and water hemlock (*Cicuta maculata;* also poisonous)

WARNING: Extremely poisonous. One of the deadliest plants on the planet. If you accidentally ingest the plant, symptoms may include salivation, nausea, coldness in the

FORAGER NOTE: The leaves of poison hemlock look much like ferns or flat-leaved parsley. Many accounts say the plant can be recognized by purple stripes or spots, but **do not rely** on this. The purple markings are not always present on poison hemlock, and other members of the carrot family also have purple markings.

extremities, respiratory failure, heart failure, paralysis, coma, and death. Contact a poison control center and get to a hospital immediately. It is always a good idea to bring a sample of what has been ingested to the hospital with you along with any photos or notes on what you think you ate.

Description

This large herbaceous biennial is a **very poisonous** member of the carrot family.

First-year basal leaves grow to about 18" long. Leaves are large, hairless, lance-shaped, and alternate, forming lacy triangles. They are deeply but delicately toothed, creating a fern-like pattern. Leaves are pinnately divided, 12"–20" long and 4"–12" wide. The leaf veins terminate at the tips of the serrated teeth (like osha).

The leaves are somewhat foul smelling (unlike wild carrot or osha leaves, which smell like carrot). But beware: The edible lookalikes are so pungent that if they are growing interspersed with poison hemlock, their overpowering scent can make everything smell like carrot.

The basal and lower leaves have long petioles; the upper leaves have shorter petioles. The base of each petiole is partially covered by a sheath.

In its second year poison hemlock grows to about 3'–10' tall.

Inflorescent umbels consist of tiny white flowers atop sturdy hollow, smooth stems that stand straight and tall. They bloom from late spring to midsummer. The compound umbels are about 2½" wide. Inflorescent clusters are found from the middle to the tops of the stalks.

Stems are hollow and branching and can have purple stripes or blotches, mostly toward the bottom. The purple markings are **not necessarily a distinguishing characteristic** of poison hemlock. Many edible species of this family also have purple stems, and these marking are not always present on poison hemlock, so additional identification must be utilized. Also, a white bloom or coating that can be wiped off with your finger covers the stem of poison hemlock; the wild carrot does not have the bloom.

Range and Habitat

Naturalized throughout most of the United States, although more sparsely in the northern, far western, and far southwestern parts of the country. Found in moist and poorly drained soils, especially along creeks, ponds, and roadside ditches. Native of North Africa, Europe, and Asia.

Comments

Poison hemlock is one of the world's most famous poisons. In 399 BC it was used to execute one of the world's most famous philosophers, Socrates. Socrates was put on trial for questioning the government and sentenced to death for doing so.

Poison hemlock contains a neurotoxin called coniine (among other poisonous components), which causes respiratory paralysis and death in humans and in many animals. I have read that artificial respiration can assist until the effects have worn off, but I sure wouldn't want to find myself in the position where this was necessary.

The plant spreads by seed and is often found in dense stands. Considered a noxious weed in some states.

The use of the word "hemlock" can be confusing because it is used for a variety of plant species and types. Hemlock is also used to describe the cicutas (water hemlocks). There's also the British member of the carrot family, *Oenanthe crocata* (called water dropwort or hemlock), which is also extremely poisonous. Because they look so similar, hemlock can also refer to edible members of the carrot family, such as *Sium suave* (called water parsnip or Hemlock water parsnip). Finally there is the tsuga, a big coniferous tree also known as hemlock.

The main thing to remember is that when it comes to the group of plants with big white umbels, be very careful. Make sure you are absolutely positive of your identification before eating anything. There are several **very poisonous members** of this lookalike group.

GOLDEN BANNER
Thermopsis spp.

Family: Fabaceae

Other names: Goldenbeans, false lupine, buffalo bean, golden pea, wet tooth, yellow bean, prairie buckbean, buffalo flower, yellow pea

Lookalikes: Perennial sweet pea, alfalfa, vetches, clovers, sweet clovers, wild licorice, lupine, spider flower

Related species: Spreadfruit golden banner (*Thermopsis divaricarpa;* straight or curved seedpods are glabrous, not hairy), mountain golden banner (*T. montana;* straight, erect seedpods), prairie golden banner (*T. rhombifolia;* strongly curved seedpods)

WARNING: Not edible; toxic. Be extremely careful about identifications. Many members of the Pea family are toxic, and many of these also have pea pods. *Do not* be tempted to eat them, even though they look like peas you would buy in a grocery store.

Description

These perennial members of the pea family grow up to 3' tall. The different species have very similar flowers, though they vary somewhat in seedpod characteristics, height, and the elevation where found.

The golden banners produce an array of showy, bright yellow pea-like flowers that are similar to other flowers in the pea family. Alternate leaves are distinctly three-lobed, although some are single and opposite.

Range and Habitat

From Washington and Montana to New Mexico. Full sun to partial shade. Moderate to high elevation. Mostly found in wooded areas and along wooded edges.

MONKSHOOD
Aconitum spp.

Family: Ranunculaceae

Other names: Wolf's bane, leopard's bane, women's bane, devil's helmet, blue rocket

Lookalikes: Larkspur, lupines, harebells, mountain bluebells, geranium (leaves), buttercup (leaves), globeflower (leaves)

Related species: Columbian monkshood (*A. columbianum*), northern/mountain monkshood (*A. delphinifolium*)

WARNING: Extremely poisonous. Do not consume in any quantity. All parts of plants contain the deadly poison aconitine. Symptoms may include paralysis of the nervous system, numbness, vomiting, diarrhea, excessive salivation, dizziness, anxiety, coma, paralysis, cardiac arrest, asphyxiation, and frequently death.

Description

This perennial is somewhat similar in appearance to the delphiniums (larkspur) but often shorter, growing 5"–5' in height (depending on species). Tall erect, smooth stalks with deeply lobed palmate leaves growing along the stalk. Some have long, narrowly divided leaves; others are more widely divided.

Blue to purple or violet (sometimes white, yellow, or pink) flowers have a distinctive upper spur and bloom in midsummer. Loose clusters of three to five flowers form a raceme along the stalk. Each flower has five petal-like sepals, the top one looking like a helmet or hood coming up and over the top of the flower.

Range and Habitat
Moist soils, open meadows, woodlands and wetlands up to subalpine and tundra zones. Found around the globe. Often found growing in the same habitats as larkspurs, but less common.

Comments
The genus name, *Aconitum,* means "unconquerable poison." Most reports say these flowers are safe to handle, although some say numbness can occur just by touching. Monkshoods seem to be used in some cultures for medicinal purposes but only after serious and careful preparations. This is definitely *not* a plant to fool around with at home.

Aconitum poison has been used in Europe, Asia, and the New World to tip arrows or spears with poison for hunting large animals—and for murdering humans.

Aconitum ferrox, a species native to Nepal, is considered the deadliest plant in the world. Just thinking about it makes my stomach flip.

BANEBERRY
Actaea rubra

Family: Ranunculaceae

Other names: Red baneberry, red cohosh, necklaceweed, snakeberry, *poison de couleuvre,* doll's eye (variation with white berries), *yerba del peco*

Lookalikes: Sweet cicely (leaves), thimbleberry (leaves), bistorts (flowers look like large bistort flowers), skunkbrush (similar berries), rose hips, and anything with a red or white berry

WARNING: Very poisonous. Do not ingest. The poisonous qualities are due to protoanemonin, a poisonous essential oil found in all parts of the baneberry plant. Ingestion causes stomach cramps, burning, headache, dizziness, vomiting, bloody diarrhea, increased pulse, and circulatory problems.

FORAGER NOTE: Berries are usually red but sometimes white. Often grows near edible sweet cicely; early in the season, their leaves can look especially similar.

Description

This native perennial has large leaves, grows in dense patches, and reaches 1'–3' tall. Stems are branched. Alternate leaves are toothed and deeply lobed. They are two to three times compound.

Long flower stems shoot upwards and produce rounded, elongated clusters of white flowers somewhat like a very large clover. Green seedpods form after the flowers fade away and mature into bright red (sometimes white) berries that stand in clusters atop erect stalks flanked by dense patches of leaves.

Range and Habitat

From Alaska to New Mexico and across the northern United States. Grows up to mid-altitude, montane, and subalpine zones. Grows in moist soils and woodlands, usually in the shade.

Comments

Don't confuse baneberry with such edible berries as thimbleberry, chokecherry, pin cherry, raspberries, and currants. While there are some limited medicinal uses for baneberry root, the berries are toxic and cannot be used as food. All parts of this plant should be considered poisonous.

LARKSPUR
Delphinium spp.

Family: Ranunculaceae

Lookalikes: Monkshood, wild geranium (leaves), lupine (flowers and, to some extent, leaves), harebells, mountain bluebells, buttercup (leaves), globeflower (leaves)

Related species: Dwarf larkspur (*D. nuttallianum*), Colorado larkspur/Alpine larkspur (*D. Alepestre*), Wahatoya Creek larkspur (*D. robustum*), Sierra larkspur/tall larkspur (*D. glaucum*), tow/little larkspur (*D. bicolor*), subalpine larkspur (*D. barbeyi*), and others

WARNING: Severely toxic. Often fatal if ingested. All parts of all delphinium species are severely poisonous. **Do not consume.** Symptoms can include muscular weakness, spasms, burning of the mouth, severe vomiting and diarrhea, weak pulse, respiratory paralysis, convulsions, and death.

Description

This herbaceous native can be annual or perennial. Larkspurs have showy spikes of blue, white, or purple terminal flower clusters. Flowers look somewhat like leaping dolphins. Leaves are palmate with pointed tips. They are deeply lobed three to seven times. Leaves are about 6"–12" long and vary in size and shape with species. Most species have widely lobed leaves; some are thinner. Stems are erect and 4"–7' tall.

Range and Habitat

Individual larkspur species often have limited ranges, but together they reach from Alaska south through Texas and across the United States to both coasts. They can be found up to about 9,500' in elevation in meadows and forest openings.

Comments

Delphinium varieties are popular in home gardens. It is wise to visit a garden nursery and have a look at their larkspurs so that you become familiar with what they look like. There are many cultivated varieties, so keep in mind that wild varieties may look somewhat different.

Herbs

YARROW
Achillea millefolium

Family: Asteraceae
Other names: Soldier's woundwort, knight's milfoil, milfoil, common yarrow, bloodwort, carpenter's weed, *hierba de las cortaduras,* plumajillo, gordaldo, nosebleed plant
Lookalikes: Poison hemlock (*Conium maculatum*), water hemlock (*Cicuta maculata*), osha (*Ligusticum porteri*), osha del campo (Angelica; *Angelica grayi*), Queen Anne's lace (*Daucus carota*), wild parsleys (*Lomatium* spp.), water parsnip (*Sium suave*)
WARNING: Do not confuse with the deadly poison hemlock or water hemlock. Yarrow leaves are distinct and with practice are very recognizable and distinguishable from the more parsley-looking leaves of the poisonous species.

Description
This perennial member of the Aster family is similar to some members of the carrot family in that its tiny flowers and florets form white umbrella-shaped clusters. Wild varieties are mostly white, but pink and yellow varieties are cultivated. Some cultivated varieties are huge, reaching 5' tall.

Conspicuous white umbels top an erect stem, 8"–2' tall. Fern-like leaves are very lacy and compact. They are alternate along the stem. Basal leaves and those lower on stem are larger that those higher up. Leaves are 2"–8" long. Flower heads are 2"–5" in diameter.

Native, with some introduced species. Yarrow flowers from spring well into late summer. After flowering, the fruits are achenes and retain much the same look as the original flower.

Range and Habitat

Yarrow grows from northern Canada to Texas and is found on sunny slopes, along roadsides, and in forest openings and disturbed areas up to 11,400' in elevation or so.

RECIPE

Poultice to Stop Bleeding

Yarrow is an important part of a wild plant first-aid kit. The leaves of yarrow can be chewed or mashed by hand to make a poultice. Place the mashed leaves on an open wound, or for a large gash, pack the bleeding opening with yarrow leaves for much faster clotting time.

RECIPE

Yarrow Tea

Yarrow leaves and flowers can be made into a tea and taken internally or poured over a wound or open sores. As a tea, it should be slowly sipped beginning about 30 minutes before meals. This slow sipping of bitters triggers the parasympathetic nervous system and helps aid in digestion and helps alleviate stress. Sipping the bitter tea will, over time, tone and strengthen the digestive system, among other benefits.

Tea can be made from fresh or dried leaves and flowers. To dry, harvest fresh leaves and flowers and hang to dry in a dark place. When crisp, store in a jar through winter.

Use 5–10 leaves per mug of tea (about 2.5 cups water). Bring water to a boil and pour over yarrow leaves. Cover and steep for 5–10 minutes. For a digestive tonic, drink ¼ cup of the warm or cooled tea slowly before mealtime. Tea can be stored in the refrigerator for several days. Excellent mixed with other ginger root, osha, honey, and peppermint.

Comments

The Latin name is derived from Achilles, the Greek warrior who used yarrow poultices to stop his soldiers from bleeding to death. It was, and still is, also widely used throughout the Rocky Mountain region as a bitter tea and as a poultice to stop bleeding.

All parts of the plant can be used for tea, but it is best to harvest the leaves and flowers, not the root, so that the perennial root system remains intact and can provide next year's harvest.

Dried, yarrow makes a sturdy ornamental flower—a great reminder of summer that can last for years.

Rub yarrow leaves on the skin for a natural bug repellent.

Harvest by removing one leaf from several different plants. Leaves can be dried and stored for winter use as tea or for your first-aid kit to stop bleeding.

PEARLY EVERLASTING
Anaphalis margaritacea

Family: Asteraceae
Other names: Western pearly everlasting

Description

This native perennial sports a tiny, delicate, papery looking flower that is notable by its showy, rounded white flower heads. A whorl of papery involucral bracts forms a flower head about ⅜" wide, often with a yellow or brownish center. Leaves are single, slender, and alternate with an obvious midvein along an erect stem that stands 4"–36" high (usually on the shorter side).

> RECIPE
>
> **Salad Greens**
>
> The leaves can also be used raw and added to salad.

This lovely plant flowers in early spring to summer, and the delicate white flowers stay almost perfect looking for months.

Range and Habitat
Found widely across the United States from Alaska to New Mexico in mid-high elevations in the mountains. Does not grow in the southernmost states. Usually seen in low-growing clumps along roadsides or disturbed areas and in forest openings. Can grow in poor soil, sand, and loam. Very cold tolerant. Hardy to minus 43°F.

Comments
Young and old leaves are edible; tender and delicious raw or cooked. The greens have a pleasant, understated flavor. For crafters, the "everlasting" nature of the flower makes this a great addition to dried-flower bouquets and wreaths. Pearly everlasting is also used as incense and as a medicinal astringent.

RECIPE

Simple Sautéed Greens

Such a delicate looking plant (although it is quite hardy) requires a simple, delicate recipe.

Briefly sauté young or old greens in a small amount of olive oil over medium heat. Remove from heat, and add a pinch of sea salt. Serve hot.

BURDOCKS
Arctium spp.

Family: Asteraceae

Other names: Edible burdock, beggar's buttons, louse bur, bardane, wild burdock, wild rhubarb, cuckoo button

Lookalikes: Common cocklebur (*Xanthium strumarium*), creeping thistle, spear thistle, nodding thistle, and other species of burdock, such as woolly burdock (*A. tomentosum*); also teasel (*Dipasacus fullonum*)

Related species: Lesser burdock/common burdock (*A. minus*), greater burdock (*A. lappa*)

WARNING: Pregnant women and diabetics should not use unless working with a skilled herbalist. When harvesting seeds, be careful about inhaling the tiny hairs, which are said to be toxic. Some people have allergic reactions.

FORAGER NOTE: Not to be confused with the similarly named docks, which are in the *Rumex* genus. Both have large, low-growing leaves, but the stalks, flowers, and seeds are totally different.

Description

This genus of nonnative biennials forms a basal rosette in its first year consisting of many large, undulating, elephant ear–like leaves that can reach up to about 2' long and 1½' wide. Leaves are dark green with woolly undersides. Lower leaves are heart shaped or ovate. Smaller leaves also grow densely along the stalks and are alternate and ovate; margins often wavy. A deep taproot can reach 1'–2' deep.

In the second year a stout, erect, grooved, branched stem emerges. The plant flowers from midsummer to fall. Flowers are purple but barely emerge from the rounded barbed or hooked bracts that surround them. Flowers with surrounding pointed bracts look like thistles. When the seedpods dry out, they do not change shape.

Arctium lappa grows somewhat taller than *A. minus* and can reach up to 6½' high. Flowers are 1"–1½" in diameter. *Arctium minus* grows 1'–5' tall. Its flowers are a little smaller, about ½"–1" wide. Also see woolly burdock (*A. tomentosum*), which is similar but with a spider web–like appearance as if covered in wool.

Common cocklebur (*Xanthium strumarium*), another large-leaved, burred herb, has maple leaf–shaped or ovular leaves and more football-shaped or tubular (not round) seedpods, which are similarly covered in hooked bracts.

Range and Habitat

Burdock grows throughout the United States in waste places, disturbed areas, forest edges, roadsides, and ditches.

Comments

The leaves, roots, stems, flowers, and seeds are edible. Roots can be eaten raw or cooked and are best in fall of the first year or the following spring (before the

RECIPE

Gobo

Gobo is a traditional Japanese recipe made with burdock root.

Harvest and clean 1 large burdock root. The skin should be removed, but it is very thin. Use a potato peeler (use a light touch, no need to dig deep) or a knife to scrape off the skin. Slice into matchstick-size pieces (about 2 cups worth). Place in a bowl of water, and agitate so that the water becomes cloudy. Change water, and repeat several times until it becomes clear. Add a drop of vinegar and soak while preparing the rest of the dish.

Slice a small carrot into matchstick-size pieces; set aside.

Heat 1 tablespoon sesame oil in a skillet to medium high. While the oil is heating, drain burdock root and add to oil once it is hot. Stir-fry for 2 to 4 minutes. Add carrots and toss in. Stir-fry for 3 minutes or so. Add 1 tablespoon mirin rice wine vinegar, 2 tablespoon sake, 1 tablespoon sugar or palm sugar, and 1½ tablespoons soy sauce. Stir-fry until liquid cooks off.

Serve hot or cold topped with a sprinkle of sesame seeds.

plant flowers). Best to harvest when the ground is moist. After it rains you will have a much easier time digging out the long roots. Use a big shovel. Roasted roots can be used like coffee and can also be dried.

Young leaves and stems are eaten raw or cooked. Stems are best peeled, and older stems are better cooked. Seeds can be eaten sprouted or soaked in water and then blended and strained to make a milk.

Burdock is widely used for a broad range of medicinal purposes and is considered good for cleansing the body's internal organs.

RECIPE

Dried Burdock Chips

Wash and peel burdock root as described above. Slice into ¼"-thick rounds. Arrange on drying rack of a food dehydrator and dry thoroughly. A food dehydrator will take 30 to 48 hours, so plan ahead.

Remove burdock rounds from dehydrator and place onto a serving platter. Top with a dollop of pesto or apricot jam and goat cheese. If using jam and goat cheese, you can place the rounds on a cookie sheet and melt cheese in oven set to broil for 3 minutes, or until the cheese is melted.

Serve warm.

HEART-LEAVED ARNICA
Arnica cordifolia

Family: Asteraceae

Other names: Leopard's bane

Lookalikes: Arrow-leaved balsam root. This is a member of the large group of yellow aster lookalikes, both lovingly and disdainfully referred to as the Damn Yellow Composites (DYCs).

WARNING: Poisonous; not edible. Arnica is not typically taken internally except under the close supervision of a skilled herbalist. It can cause severe blistering of the throat, digestive tract, internal organs, and skin. **Use extreme caution.** Do not use salves made from this plant on open wounds.

Description

Herbaceous native perennial. Leaves are opposite along the stalk but can become alternate toward the top of the stalk just below the flower. Leaves are either lance shaped or heart shaped. Flowers are typical of the DYCs. They are bright yellow and somewhat resemble both wild sunflowers and dandelions.

Heart-leaved arnica, the most common species, grows from about 4"–2' tall.

Arnica Oil

This is very potent and is provided for informational purposes only. Do not try at home.

Harvest basal leaves of arnica (can also use flowers if available). Dry in a cool dark place on screen racks or in a paper or cloth bag. If drying in a bag, shake daily or more frequently to ensure adequate airflow. When leaves are crisp and dry, place in blender or clean coffee grinder and pulverize into a powder. You can also crush by hand or with a mortar and pestle.

Combine ¾ cup dried arnica with 2 cups good oil, such as organic olive or sesame oil. Close lid and store in a dark place; a cupboard is fine. Every day shake the mixture by gently turning the jar upside down. Allow the oil and arnica to mix and trade places, and turn over again. Do this several times. Let sit for a month or longer. Filter the arnica out with a fine sieve. Rub the oil on arthritic joints, areas of chronic inflammation (like for chronic neck pain) or areas of acute injuries, such as a sprain or bruise.

NOTE: Plant strength will vary. Some salves will be much stronger than others. If you are healthy and strong, try some on yourself under controlled circumstances (at home, not on the trail) to make sure it does not cause blisters. If you are ill, elderly, or pregnant, find a healthy adult to test the salve on for strength. If it causes blisters or skin irritation, dilute with additional oil.

Heart-leaved arnica is named for the long, heart-shaped basal leaves. The plant reproduces both by seed and roots as a spreading perennial. It flowers sporadically from different root nodes in June to July. Other arnica species flower from multi-branching herbaceous stems.

Leafy arnica (*A. chamissonis*) grows from 8" to more than 3' tall and has five to ten pairs of leaves. It prefers moister habitat than other species.

Range and Habitat

Found from the Yukon to New Mexico, from the foothills up to subalpine slopes. Heart-leaved arnica is common and grows in moist shade or dappled shade, especially in pine and aspen groves. Found from about 4,000' in the more northern regions (beginning higher in southern region) up to timberline.

Comments

Not edible. Not for internal use. Use extreme caution. External use also can be hazardous.

One herbalist that I consulted with thought arnica should be included in the poisonous plants section rather than in the useful plants section. I have included it here only because it is such a well known species and widely purchased as an ingredient in commercial salves and lotions for sore muscles and arthritis. I wanted to introduce readers to the fact that arnica is a common wild plant in our region. However, using this plant is for advanced wild crafters **only**. Attempt use **only** after taking classes and consulting personally with an experienced wild crafter.

All parts of the plant can be used for salves, but salves should be used with extreme caution and **only** on unbroken skin. Arnica dilates blood vessels and helps reduce swelling.

Arnica is typically one of the early pioneers to reemerge after forest fires.

NODDING THISTLE
Carduus nutans

Family: Asteraceae

Other names: Musk thistle, nodding plumeless thistle, *chardon penché,* plumeless thistle, thistle, milk thistle

Description

This biennial plant produces a rosette of narrow, spiny leaves 11"–23" long in the spring or summer of its first year. By mid-spring of the second year, branched stems will emerge from the rosette. In warmer climates the entire life cycle will sometimes be completed in one year. Leaves are waxy, dark green and coarsely lobed, with sharp yellowish, brownish, or whitish spines at the tips of the lobes.

Reaches 3'–5' tall. Stems are hairy, spiny, branched, and smoother toward the top. The top portion of the stems and branches may host a few spines that

FORAGER NOTE: Flower heads are notable by the very large bracts below the flowering portion that resemble an artichoke. The name nodding thistle comes from another notable characteristic: Instead of standing erect, the flower heads typically nod downwards up to 90 degrees or more, especially as they mature.

are much smaller than those along the bottom two-thirds of the stalks. The very spiny leaves also become more sparse, or absent, toward the top.

Spherical flower heads 1"–3" in diameter are notable by the very large bracts below the flowering portion. It resembles its relative, the artichoke. Each plant produces anywhere from one to fifty flower heads in late spring to late summer. Each flower can produce over 1,000 seeds, which are fluffy, dispersed by wind (although they often don't make it very far), and can remain viable for more than a decade. Flower heads droop 90 to 120 degrees once mature, less droopy when young.

Range and Habitat
From British Columbia to Texas and from coast to coast. Found from sea level to about 8,500' in elevation or higher. Nodding thistle grows on disturbed sites, meadows, and pastures with moderate moisture and prefer full sun. They do not grow well in shade.

Comments
Can be eaten like other thistles. Peel stem and eat the young, still soft part—not the woody inner stem. Considered helpful for liver function.

RECIPE

Boiled Stem

Remove spines as describe for other thistles. Gently peel the outer layer of the young stem. Boil for a few minutes until soft. Douse with truffle oil or butter and a bit of tamari or salt.

CHICORY
Cichorium intybus

Family: Asteraceae
Other names: Wild endive, French endive, succory, blue sailors, coffee weed
Lookalikes: Blue flax, especially from afar

Description

Nonnative biennial or perennial. This scraggly, somewhat branched weed grows 1½'–3' tall. Toward its base, lots of large, unlobed, dandelion-like leaves up to

> ### RECIPE
>
> **Chicory Coffee**
>
> Strong-tasting dark beverage, usually consumed hot.
>
> Harvest roots and let dry. When you are ready to make a beverage, grind the root finely as you would coffee beans. Dry roast on a thick skillet or cast iron pan until just browning. Use in French press or a slow-drip coffeemaker. Fix as you would coffee.

about 8" long. Leaves become much smaller upwards along the stalk. Known for its large taproot.

Iridescent blue flowers (rarely pink or white) scattered along the thin stalks, often bobbing in the wind. Inflorescences are up to about 1½" across. Flowers mid- to late summer and into fall. Each petal has five tiny grooves along the blunt outer edges, creating a small wave effect.

Range and Habitat

From British Columbia across North America to Florida. Roadsides and disturbed areas.

RECIPE

Garlic Fava Beans and Chicory Greens

Prepare 1 cup fava beans by soaking in water overnight. Rinse well and then simmer (do not boil) in a large pot until soft. Drain and set aside. Retain the bean water.

In a large pot combine 2 cups of the bean water, 5 cloves garlic, chopped, and 2 bay leaves. Bring to a boil. Add 2 cups chopped chicory leaves and reduce heat to a low simmer. Simmer for 10 minutes. Add the cooked fava beans and simmer 5 to 10 more minutes. Remove from heat, and toss with salt and pepper to taste.

Variation: If the leaves are too bitter, first boil in clear water for 5 to 10 minutes; then drain and proceed with recipe.

Comments

A relative of the endive. Listed as a noxious weed in Colorado.

To cultivate chicory to mimic store-bought light-colored endives, cut the plant short and cover with a basket to prevent sunlight from reaching the plant for photosynthesis. Once leaves appear, they will be blanched (white) and tender.

Roots can also be dug up, dried, and used as a diuretic for medicinal purposes or as a strong tea or coffee-like (but caffeine-free) drink. Green leaves can also be eaten. Many people find them bitter, which can be reduced by boiling leaves in a few changes of water.

CREEPING THISTLE/CANADA THISTLE
Cirsium arvense

Family: Asteraceae
Other names: Canadian thistle, California thistle, field thistle, lettuce from hell thistle, cursed thistle, prickly thistle, small-flowered thistle, way thistle
Lookalikes: Sow thistle, burdock, Bigelow's tansy aster *(Machaeranthera bigelovii)*
Related species: Bull thistle (*C. vulgare*), Hooker's thistle (*C. hookerianum*), leafy thistle (*C. foliosum*)

Description
This creeping perennial, lavender or pink-purple flowered member of the Aster family, reproduces both by spreading root systems and by seed. Inflorescences are nicely scented, up to about 1¼" wide and long. Bracts are not spiny or prickly like so many other thistles.

FORAGER NOTE: Shorter than the bull thistle, without the prolific spines.

Flowers appear in clusters at the top of the stalks. Florets are similar (not divided into ray and disc florets). Creeping thistle flowers in late spring or early summer and sometimes again throughout the season, depending on the conditions. By late summer or fall, it gives way to a white and feathery pappus (like a dandelion when it goes to seed).

Its erect, branching, smooth stems grow 1'–4' tall. Stems may become hairy as they age. Leaves are alternate and spiny and grow 3"–8" long along the stalk. Leaves are larger toward the bottom and smaller toward the top of the stem.

The extensive root systems will produce new shoots when tilled or broken. They extend 6'–15' deep and can grow more than 15' horizontally. Seeds, especially when deeply buried, remain viable for more than twenty years. Seven hundred to 1,500 (or more) seeds are produced per stem.

Two main factors distinguish *C. arvense* from other thistles: Male and female flowers are on separate plants, and dense patches are formed by the spreading root systems, hence the name creeping thistle. Compared to the spiny-stemmed bull thistle (*Cirsium vulgare*) and nodding thistle (*Carduus nutans*), Canada thistle stems are **not** spiny.

Range and Habitat

Hardy to USDA Zone 4. The common name Canada thistle is misleading, as this species is actually a European native. It is found widely from Alaska to New

Mexico and California to the East Coast where there is moderate moisture. It is considered a noxious weed in most states because it thrives on sunny pastureland and other stressed and disturbed environments, where it decreases range habitat for cattle. A 1998 study showed that in Colorado alone, about 400,000 acres were "infested" with Canada thistle.

Does not survive in shade or healthy, diverse ecosystems. Hummingbirds hope state eradication programs are unsuccessful, as they use thistle fluff to build their tiny nests. Honeybees also rely on creeping thistle and are a main pollinator of it.

Comments

Roots, leaves, stems, and young flowers are edible. Young, still-flexible stalks can be eaten raw or cooked. Especially good to harvest when the plant is 1' tall or less. The roots can also be used as food and medicine. De-spine leaves before eating. Roots can be used medicinally to support the liver.

This is a very common weed throughout the United States. The plant reproduces readily, so feel free to harvest. Many farmers, private citizens, and government entities regularly poison stands of thistle, so harvesting for your own use will also help prevent the continued use of poisonous herbicides. Of course make sure you are gathering **prior** to any chemical eradication efforts, or check with local farmers to see how you can devise a symbiotic relationship.

SPEAR THISTLE/BULL THISTLE
Cirsium vulgare

Family: Asteraceae
Other names: Scotch thistle, common thistle, prickly vase, Fuller's thistle
Lookalikes: Plumeless thistle (*Carduus acanthoides*), which lacks a prominent midrib on leaves; Scotch thistle (*Onopordum acanthium/O. tauricum*)

Description
This tall biennial European immigrant has solitary flowers atop spiny branches. Flowers are rose-purplish, lavender, purple, and sometimes white and 1"–2" wide. Inflorescences are not divided into ray and disc florets but are all similar.

FORAGER NOTE: Stems are winged with spines, and the entire plant is covered in spines. Distinguishable from creeping thistle because bull thistle is not only covered in spikes but also forms a basal rosette, which its perennial relative does not.

Lightly Boiled Flower Buds

Harvest 2 cups young flower buds before they open. Bring medium-size pot of lightly salted water to a boil. Add buds and boil for 10 minutes; drain. Serve as a side dish with grilled black bean burgers.

The entire plant—leaves, stems, and branches—is covered in spines and prickers all the way up to the bracts (base of the flower head).

The first-year basal rosette is formed by deeply lobed and very spiny leaves 3"–6" long. In the second year a many-branched stem 5'–6' tall will emerge, with flowers clustering at the tops. The stem and branches are winged with spines. Leaves are more prominent along the stem and its base, becoming progressively smaller toward the top of the stalk.

Seeds have a feathery pappus and are wind dispersed. Seeds remain viable for only a few years and usually germinate quickly.

Range and Habitat

Hardy to USDA Zone 2. Found on disturbed sites, including pastureland, over-grazed ranges, forest clear-cuts, roadsides, and ditches from Alaska to Texas. It is uncommon in ungrazed grasslands.

An early-successional species. Requires sun; does not grow in shade.

Taproot and Fresh Greens Stew

Carefully harvest starchy taproot. Look for basal rosettes in the fall, and harvest carefully with thick gloves and a big shovel. Remove leaves, and scrub root with water and a stiff brush to remove dirt. Chop root into 2" pieces.

Add to slow cooker with 4 carrots, 1 large yam, and 1 large turnip, all chopped into about 2" pieces. Fill slow cooker three-quarters full with water. Add 3 bay leaves, ½ jalapeño, and ½ teaspoon each salt and pepper. Add ½ cup barley. Cook until bubbling and all ingredients are soft.

To serve, place 1 cup chopped kale and mizuna in each bowl. Spoon hot stew on top of the fresh greens. Enjoy as is, or garnish with fresh-chopped herbs such as basil, parsley, or mint.

Variations: Add 1 cup chopped chicken. Add several vegan or chicken bullion cubes.

Comments

Flowers, buds, leaves, roots, stem, seeds, and oil are edible but somewhat bland flavored. Good to mix into more flavorful dishes. Young stems can be cooked like asparagus. Leaves can be soaked in salt water and then cooked. Root can be dried or cooked. Flowers and buds are good cooked. Seeds can be roasted and eaten.

Bull thistles are full of nectar and provide food for honeybees, bumblebees, hummingbirds, and butterflies. Seeds are eaten by American goldfinches, juncos, mice, and many other birds and rodents.

FLEABANE
Erigeron spp.

Family: Asteraceae
Other names: Fleabane daisy, fleawort
Lookalikes: Asters, daisies, symphyotrichum
Related species: Many, including featherleaf fleabane (*E. pinnatisectus*), Canada fleabane (*E. canadensis*), common fleabane (*E. philadelphicus*)
WARNING: See comments below. Might not be right for all people.

Description
This group of perennial natives has about 170 species in North America. They are difficult to tell apart, but all are low growing and often found in spreading clusters. Fleabanes have short, hairy stems and can grow up to 3' tall for some species. Often seen in the range of 4"–8" high.

Leaves are small, alternate, and lance shaped but vary with species. Some species have leaves that clump toward the bottom of the stalk; others climb the stalk more evenly. Featherleaf fleabane has more feathery, deeply divided leaves.

Flowers consists of fifty to one hundred narrow lavender or purple petals arranged in a sunburst shape around a yellow center.

Range and Habitat

Roadsides, fields, and openings up to about 13,000' in elevation for some species. Common fleabane is found from the Yukon throughout most of the United States. Featherleaf fleabane has a limited range and is found in the mountains of Wyoming, Colorado, and New Mexico.

Comments

We Americans have a fairly basic relationship with the food we eat. Foraging provides a means to dramatically deepen that relationship. While fleabane is generally considered edible, it may not be appropriate for all people at all times. The rule of thumb has been described to me like this: First taste a very small amount of raw fleabane. If it tastes good to you raw, you can eat more. If it does not taste good, then you should not eat it. This test should be conducted each time you wish to eat fleabane.

Leaves and sprouts are edible cooked. They also can be dried and cooked later. Can be dried and burned as a smudge to cleanse the house and repel insects. Can be made into an oil for the same purpose.

Many lookalike species. Known for repelling fleas and other bugs.

COMMON SUNFLOWER
Helianthus annuus

Family: Asteraceae

WARNING: Some people are allergic to members of the Asteraceae family.

Description
This tall, showy, erect native annual stands 4'–12' high or higher. In 2009, *Guinness World Records* recognized a German *Helianthus annus* as the tallest ever recorded at 26' 4".

Large, yellow (sometimes red or orange) terminal inflorescences are a composite of hundreds of flowers arranged in a large disc and ray floret pattern. The

Raw Sunflower Seed Milk

Collect a pint glass full of sunflower seeds. Remove the shells by gently crushing them. For assistance separating seeds from shells, soak cracked seeds in water and allow shells to float to the top. Skim shells off with a tea strainer and agitate the water, allowing more shells to be freed to float up. Once shells are removed, soak seeds in a bowl of fresh water for 8 hours. Change the water once or twice during that time.

Rinse seeds, and place in blender. Fill blender with water, and blend on high speed until water is white and milky and seeds are pulverized, about 3 minutes. Strain through a very fine sieve, making sure to collect the milk in a bowl below. Use a soft spatula to press all the milk out. Use as a milk replacement; great with muesli or granola and dried fruit.

Store in a glass jar with a lid in the fridge for five to seven days. Save seed pulp for Sunflower Seed Granola (see recipe below). The milk will separate and needs to be shaken before each use.

Variations: Add honey for a sweeter milk. Add a few dates (pits removed) for sweetness and thickness. Substitute raw almonds for half the sunflower seeds.

outer ring of petals is yellow; the inner ring is brown or brownish yellow. The flower head is smaller than the cultivated varieties, measuring about 5" across. The tiny flowers on the inner part of the inflorescence create a fractal-like spiral pattern. Blooms late summer to early fall.

Seeds are also smaller than commercial sunflower seeds but otherwise look similar, with a blackish outer shell and succulent seed inside.

The leaves are hairy. Lower leaves are often heart shaped and opposite. Leaves along the stalk are more egg shaped or oblong and alternate. The stout, erect stem is branched many times and hairy. Usually found in large stands.

Range and Habitat
Found in open, often disturbed areas in the plains and foothills. Up to about 9,000' in elevation. This common and widespread bundle of sunshine is actually considered a weed in many states.

Comments
Flowers, seeds, and the oil are edible. The oils from the seeds are rich in linoleic acid. Young flower buds can be eaten, often steamed. Seeds can be eaten raw, roasted, dried, or crushed and mixed with other foods.

The leaves can also be crushed and used as a poultice and can also be used as tea for a variety of medicinal purposes. Flowers can be made into medicinal tea, and root decoctions are also used as medicine.

Wild sunflower was cultivated by Native Americans, who selected plants for larger and larger seed size. The USDA reports that such cultivation led to an increase in seed size of about 1,000 percent.

RECIPE

Sunflower Seed Granola

Using the pulp from the milk recipe above, combine with an equal amount dry organic oats, ⅛ cup flax seeds, and 2 tablespoons soft coconut oil or butter. Mix well. Add lots of plump fat raisins; combine. Spray a cookie sheet with oil. Press mixture onto cookie sheet until about ¼" to ¾" thick. Bake at 225°F until just beginning to brown around the edges, about 30 minutes, but this will vary depending on your oven, how thick your mixture is pressed out, and altitude. Continue baking another 5 to 8 minutes. Remove from oven and let cool. Break into pieces, and store in a glass jar with a lid. Use like cereal; serve with fresh almond or sunflower seed milk.

Variation: Dry in a food dehydrator rather than in the oven.

CHAMOMILE
Matricaria spp.

Family: Asteraceae
Other names: Wild chamomile
Lookalikes: Stinking chamomile (*Anthemis cotula*)
Related species: German chamomile/scented mayweed (*M. recutita, M. chamomilla*), Scentless mayweed/scentless chamomile (*M. inodora, M. perforata, Tripleurospermum perforatum*)
WARNING: Not safe for pregnant women. Can cause contractions of the uterus. A ragweed relative, it can cause an allergic reaction, especially in those allergic to ragweed. It has been reported to cause anaphylactic shock, although most people enjoy chamomile with no problems. Mild sedative effect.

Description
This nonnative Eurasian annual or perennial (depending on species) looks like much smaller, clumping shasta daisies with feathery leaves. Low-lying clumps of lovely daisy-like white flowers on spindly stems. Ray petals are white surrounding an upward-pushing, prominent yellow central disc. Leaves are very deeply lobed into thin, wispy leaf divisions. Leaves appear delicate and feathery. Grows

from 6"–2' tall. Scented mayweed smells like honey or apples. Scentless chamomile is not strongly scented.

Range and Habitat

M. indora is found from Alaska and across Canada down to Nevada, Utah, and Colorado and across some of the northeastern states. Does not appear to be found in California or Oregon. *M. recutita* is found sporadically throughout the Rockies. Sunny, disturbed areas throughout the temperate zone.

RECIPE

Chamomile Mint Tea

For a pot of tea, harvest several flower heads and a few sprigs of wild mint. Wash and place in tea strainer. Boil water, and pour over fresh herbs. Place lid on top of strainer and let steep 10 minutes. Add generous amounts of fresh local honey, and stir well. Serve hot, or enjoy lukewarm throughout the day.

    Variation: Use dried herbs.

RECIPE

Chamomile Eye Pillow

This works best with the scented mayweed (*M. recutita*).

Harvest 1 cup flowers, and dry in a dark place.

Find a nice soft fabric with relaxing colors, and cut it into two 8½ x 3½-inch rectangles. Place the rectangles so that the edges match up and the outside of the fabric for each piece is facing inward. Sew the two long edges and one short edge using a tight stitch. Then pull the sewn edges through so that the pillow is no longer inside out. Gently fill the pillow through the open end with the dried flowers. Sew the remaining edge closed.

At bedtime lie on your back in a comfortable position that allows your shoulders, neck, and back to relax. Place the eye pillow over your eyes and focus on breathing deeply in and out. Allow the gentle scent of chamomile to waft over you as you drift to sleep.

Comments

Well known as a relaxing tea, good for digestion and as a mild sleep aid. The stalk, leaves, and flowers can be used. Chamomile has a variety of medicinal uses and can be made into cosmetics such as shampoo and oils. Always steep tea covered to retain the beneficial aromatics.

Lookalike stinking chamomile (*Anthemis cotula*) is found widely across the United States and has a strong smell.

PINEAPPLE WEED
Matricaria discoidea

Family: Asteraceae

Other names: Disc mayweed

Lookalikes: Feathery leaves and yellow flower can be confused with chamomile. Pineapple weed is much smaller and lacks the white daisy-like petals of chamomile.

WARNING: Some people are allergic to this plant. If you are allergic to ragweed or other asters, take caution. Has a mild sedative effect on some people.

Description
Small, pungent annual ground cover grows 2"–16" high but is more commonly 4"–8" high. Pineapple weed has hairless, branched stems and alternate, feathery leaves ⅛"–2" long. Inflorescences are pineapple-scented yellow or light greenish cone-shaped discs that do not have petals.

Range and Habitat
This Eurasian native now grows from Alaska to New Mexico on disturbed, compacted soil. Likes full sun. Blooms in spring to late spring and withers in the heat of July. Will sometimes reemerge in August as the weather cools.

Liz and Rich's Wedding Tea

When my husband and I got married in our backyard in July 2010, we had a profusion of pineapple weed growing, especially around the newly laid flagstone. It was amazingly delicious to walk through the burgeoning garden, because the sweet scent of crushed pineapple weed underfoot joined you for a stroll. Many wedding ceremonies include the couple sipping wine out of a goblet. We decided to make our own sun tea out of edible plants growing around us and save the wine drinking for later. Next to the chuppa that we built, we set up a table with all the things that would be used throughout the ceremony.

We filled a clear glass mason jar one-third full with herbs including pineapple weed, mint, raspberry leaves, and wild rose flowers all from our yard. We filled the jar with water and tightened the lid. It sat in the sun for two days before it was used to seal the deal.

I highly recommend enjoying your pineapple weed sun tea with friends and family, and sealing it with a kiss and a killer party.

Comments

The leaves are sweet and leave the tongue feeling a bit minty. The flower heads are delicately pineapple flavored.

CUTLEAF CONEFLOWER
Rudbeckia laciniata

Family: Asteraceae
Other names: Tall coneflower, green-head coneflower
Lookalikes: Black-eyed Susan, sunflower
WARNING: Do not use during pregnancy.

Description
Tall showy native grows from 3'–8' tall. Hairless, erect stems with large leaves that are deeply lobed and coarsely toothed, forming really interesting shapes. Leaves can be huge, up to about 12" long, with three to seven graceful lobed cutouts. Usually found in clusters that form from underground rhizomes.

Large yellow ray flowers surround greenish-yellow (sometimes brownish) center button of disc florets. Yellow petal-like ray flowers surround the central disc. Flower heads are up to about 3" in diameter.

Range and Habitat

Mountains of the four-corners states and Wyoming and into Canada and the eastern United States; not found wild in the West Coast states. Grows in especially moist areas with rich soil, such as streambanks and ditches, from about 5,000'–8,500' in elevation or higher.

Comments

Especially attractive to birds and bees, including honeybees.

Generally thought to be more actively medicinal than black-eyed Susan. Roots used as a substitute for echinacea. Make a decoction of the roots, and drink as a medicinal tea at onset of illness.

A very few sources claim that young shoots, stalks, and leaves are edible raw or cooked. Most people do not have experience eating them, and I have not confirmed their edibility.

Flowers can also be made into a yellow dye.

NOTE: This is not well known as an edible plant. Many consider it medicinal only.

GOLDENRODS
Solidago spp.

Family: Asteraceae

Related species: Rocky Mountain goldenrod (*S. multiradiata*), baby goldenrod (*S. nana*), Canada goldenrod (*S. canadensis*), giant goldenrod (*S. gigantea*), Missouri goldenrod (*S. missouriensis*)

WARNING: Some people are allergic to goldenrod. Try very small amounts at first.

Description

Erect perennial herb from 7"–2' tall. (Giant goldenrod reaches more than 8' tall.) Stems can be green or reddish and are often branched. Usually smooth, in some species the stems are hairy. Leaves can be smooth or fuzzy, depending on species. Often grows in small or large, dense patches, giving it a look similar to a yellow-flowered shrub like a baby rabbitbrush. On closer inspection, though, it is obviously several flower stalks growing densely together rather than a single shrub.

Goldenrod Leaf Gallo Pinto

Rice and beans is a household staple. I love having a well-spiced bowl full ready and waiting at meal or snack time. Cooking up a big pot has been a periodic Sunday-evening tradition ever since my husband and I visited Nicaragua, where a version of this dish is a national favorite. I can never get mine to taste quite as good, but here's my version.

Begin preparing this dish one day in advance by soaking 1 cup pinto beans in water. Place beans in a large bowl. Fill with room-temperature water, and cover with a dark cloth. Change the water twice throughout the day and once more right before you go to bed. Do this by straining the water out, rinsing the beans well until they do not foam, and then refilling the bowl with water.

Cook 1 to 2 cups white or brown rice in a rice cooker.

Bring a large pot of water to a boil; reduce to a low simmer. Meanwhile drain and rinse the beans. Add beans to simmering water. Keep a close eye on the beans, making sure they never come to a rolling boil. Maintain a slow simmer. This prevents the skin from cracking and the beans from becoming waterlogged. Cook, stirring occasionally, for about 1 hour, or until beans are soft. Drain, but retain the cooking water.

In a blender combine about one-fourth of the cooked beans and ⅔ cup of the cooking liquid. Blend on high until the mixture is just liquefied. Some remaining chunks are fine; they will add a nice texture to the dish.

In a large pot heat 2 tablespoons organic vegetable oil to medium. Add 1 jalapeno, 1 onion, and 5 cloves garlic, all chopped. Sauté until tender, about 8 minutes. Add the blended bean mixture and 1 cup roughly chopped goldenrod leaves. Stir well. Bring to a simmer, and cook until leaves are tender, about 4 minutes. Add the beans and rice. Stir gently to combine. Add salt and pepper to taste. Cook for 10 more minutes to combine flavors. Serve immediately, or store in fridge for up to one week. Delicious hot or at room temperature.

Leaves are alternate and linear and can be smooth or serrated along the margins.

Tiny yellow flowers with a central disc and outer rays form rounded or pyramidal tufts at the top of the stems. Flowers are often densely clustered, but in Canadian goldenrod, for example, they can appear leggier and form a less dense cluster.

Range and Habitat
Widely dispersed throughout the continent. While various species are restricted to certain regions, together they cover much of North America. Found along

roadsides, disturbed areas, woodland openings, alpine meadows, and tundra. Baby goldenrod is found in a more limited range: from Idaho and Montana to New Mexico and Arizona. Rocky Mountain goldenrod is found in the western half of the United States and throughout Canada.

RECIPE

Goldenrod Seed Chicken Soup

Make a good homemade chicken soup by simmering a whole farm-fresh chicken with carrots, celery, garlic, onion, bay leaves, and salt and pepper for about 6 hours, or until the broth is reduced and delicious. Strain the old vegetables, meat, and bones out of the broth.

Put broth back into soup pot. Add goldenrod seeds to thicken soup. Add fresh carrots and celery, and simmer. Pick meat from bones, and add to simmering soup. Serve hot with rice, bread, or a hot potato. Garnish with chopped fresh parsley or fresh thyme.

Comments

There are about seventy-five species of goldenrod. Flowers, seeds, leaves, and fruits are edible raw, cooked, or dried. Also can be used to make dye by soaking and boiling flowers.

DANDELION
Taraxacum officinale

Family: Asteraceae
Other names: Common dandelion
Lookalikes: Salsify (flowers), cat's ear (leaves, but cat's ear leaves are hairy), and chicory (leaves)

Description
Dandelions are thought to be introduced, but some accounts say there were pre-Columbian varieties on this continent as well.

This very common perennial grows about 2"–2' high. A sturdy taproot, 3"–8" long, produces a basal rosette of leaves, each 2"–16" long. Taproot can become branched as it ages.

Leaves are oblong and extremely variable. They are quite a bit longer than they are wide. Leaves can be decumbent or erect. They can be lobeless or lobed, often very deeply lobed. Lobes can be rounded or jagged.

Solitary yellow ray flower clusters of 100 to 300 tiny flowers (that together look like one terminal flower head) stand atop smooth, hollow stems. Flower heads are 1"–2" wide. Yellow rays are longer toward the outer edges, and most are delicately jagged at the flattish outer tips. Flower color is more or less uniform but can be somewhat darker toward the center of the inflorescence.

Flowers turn to white fluff balls that are assisted by the wind in seed dispersal. Dandelions contain white, milky latex that will ooze out when the plant is cut.

Range and Habitat
Everywhere, especially disturbed areas, burned forests, old fields and pastures, roadsides, gardens, lawns, and avalanche zones from sea level to 13,500' in elevation. Thrive in rich soils and in full sun, but survive in a very wide range of habitats.

Comments
Leaves, flowers, buds, young stalks, and roots are edible raw or cooked. Dandelions are bitter, but often pleasantly so. Best to pick leaves before the flowers appear. Leaves are somewhat less bitter when young but can be eaten when older as well. Tight, unfurled crowns, at ground level in the middle of the rosette, are also tender and edible. To best enjoy the flowers, remove them from the green bracts, although this isn't necessary.

Roots are best eaten when they are young enough to be uniformly whitish throughout, except for the darker skin. Older roots become tougher and darker in the center. Both old and younger roots can be roasted and used for dandelion "coffee."

Fresh Greens Salad

I like to prepare hardy wild greens in what I call "salad seviche." There's no fish, but the preparation is similar.

Prepare an oil-and-vinegar salad dressing. Combine 1 tablespoon olive oil, ½ tablespoon vinegar, and the juice of 1 fresh lemon or lime. Add a splash of soy sauce. Mix well until emulsified.

Wash and then chop 4 cups dandelion greens. Place greens in bowl, and pour dressing over them. Toss well. Set aside and allow to sit for 30 minutes. Just as the vinegar and citrus "cook" raw fish in the Spanish dish seviche, the combination also tenderizes the hardy greens, making them more tender and enjoyable to eat. Just before serving, toss in about 4 cups lettuce of your choice.

Variation: Add pan-fried strips of grass-fed steak.

Used to make tea, tonics, and salads and in cooked dishes. Boiling and other cooking methods can help reduce the bitterness. Mixing dandelions with other foods, especially strong-tasting foods, helps make them really enjoyable.

Dandelion wine is a well-loved tradition. My friend Michelle's family traditionally made dandelion wedding wine when a child turned 12 years old. The assumption was that in just a few years, at about age 19, there would be a wedding at which to drink it. When we were in school together in Vermont, I was lucky enough to sample this old family tradition, and it was an excellent introduction to wild crafting of wines.

Bacon Fried Young Greens

This is a very hardy breakfast, good before a day of serious lumberjacking.

Harvest 1 cup young dandelion shoots, stalks, and leaves; wash in cool water to remove any dirt. Chop roughly into strips, and steam in a steamer about 7 minutes until just wilted; set aside.

Cook some good-quality bacon in a heavy skillet. When bacon begins to crisp, remove it and set aside, leaving about 2 tablespoons of the bacon grease in the pan.

Add the steamed greens to the skillet, and pan-fry on high heat until just beginning to crisp but not burn. Remove from heat; add crumbled bacon and a bit of fresh-ground black pepper. Serve on a big bed of warm rice with a dash of soy sauce and a sprinkle of flax seeds.

Dandelions are available from the very beginning of spring to the very end of fall. One of the first flowers to open in spring and therefore one of the first foods available each year for both insects and humans. Keep this in mind and, when harvesting in early spring, leave plenty of flowers for the pollinators. Roots can be harvested throughout the winter.

Important food source for cattle, sheep, grouse, gophers, bears, deer, elk, and bees.

SALSIFY
Tragopogon dubius

Family: Asteraceae
Other names: Common goat's beard, yellow salsify, oyster plant, western salsify
Lookalikes: Dandelion, grasses
Related species: Meadow salsify (*T. pratensis*), oyster plant (*T. porrifolius*)

Description

This biennial (sometimes annual) European native looks like a tall scraggly dandelion with slightly larger flowers, although its grass-like leaves are easily distinguishable. In their first year leaves are grass-like rosettes that grow to about 14" long. In the second year a smooth flowering stalk 1'–3' high arises, sending out two to thirty smooth branches, each of which terminates in a composite flower head.

A white latex that turns to brown exudes from broken leaves. The leaves are long and deeply folded down the center, creating an obvious, somewhat-rigid V shape, like grass but much deeper. The leaves along the stem are alternate, linear, and clasping (attached directly to the stalk without a petiole).

Flowers in spring or summer. Showy yellow dandelion-like inflorescences are born singly and are ray floret composites, with the outer rays longer. Flowers are

dandelion yellow (sometimes pale lemon), about 1½" wide. The inner rays are flecked with darker brown markings and surrounded by markedly longer, thin pointed bracts (leaf-like structures just below and cupping the flower head), giving the flower heads a unique look. (Meadow salsify does not have these extended bracts.)

Seeds are attached to white fluffy pappus like a dandelion and become big white fluff balls in mid- to late summer.

A related species, *T. porrifolius,* has purple flowers and is also edible.

Range and Habitat

From Alaska to Texas in dry, disturbed sites and roadsides; a common garden weed. Found throughout the plains and foothill communities.

Comments

Salsify is one of the first plants that allowed me to realize that wild edibles can provide a superior culinary experience. With salsify, there is no grinning and bearing it while reminding yourself that it's healthy.

RECIPE

Trifecta Salsify Sampler

A real dinner party crowd pleaser. Perfect in spring or early summer.

Harvest flower buds before they have opened. Also harvest leaves and stalks. Rinse all thoroughly in water, and gently pat dry.

Separate buds from stalks. Remove leaves from stalks and make three piles: buds, leaves, and stalks. Gently steam stalks, and place on plate. Sauté leaves for just a few minutes in olive oil. Sprinkle good salt on top. Place on plate with stalks. Garnish with raw or steamed flower buds. Serve hot or at room temperature.

Variation: Drizzle truffle oil or hollandaise sauce over final product.

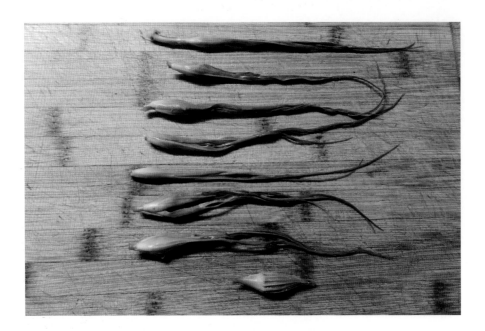

Flowers, buds, leaves, roots, and young stalks can be eaten raw, steamed, sautéed, or baked. Sweet and tender, like an artichoke heart or an oyster. Best when young; the stalk gets hard after the flowers have gone to seed.

This is a common garden weed and definitely worth cultivating.

RECIPE

Salsify Leaves Pasta Primavera

Substitute salsify leaves for the pasta in your favorite recipe.

Harvest 4 cups leaves; wash and set aside. Prepare the following vegetables by chopping into bite-size pieces: 1 zucchini, 1 yellow summer squash, 1 cup broccoli, and 1 cup cauliflower. Place in a 9 x 13" baking dish with 2 cups cherry tomatoes. Toss with enough olive oil to lightly coat the veggies; add 1 teaspoon salt. Roast in oven at 375°F until veggies are soft, about 45 minutes.

Meanwhile bring a pot of water to a boil. Boil salsify leaves for 5 minutes; drain.

To serve, line plates or serving bowl with the boiled leaves. Top with roasted vegetables. Sprinkle with a handful of pine nuts and plenty of fresh ground black pepper. Add parmesan cheese if desired.

Variation: For a raw pasta salad, simply use all the listed ingredients, but do not cook. Toss well with an olive oil, vinegar, and tahini dressing. Allow to sit in dressing for 10–30 minutes before serving.

HERBS: DOCKS AND SORRELS

ALPINE SORREL
Oxyria digyna

Family: Polygonaceae
Other names: Alpine mountain sorrel, mountain sorrel
Lookalikes: Sheep sorrel (*Rumex acetosella*) has similar flowers and seeds but different leaves. Also, alpine sheep sorrel/fewleaved dock (*Rumex paucifolius*).
WARNING: See oxalates discussion in introduction.

Description
This native perennial looks like the docks but is much smaller. It is similar to sheep sorrel in size but with different leaves and fatter, fleshier flowers and seedpods.

Fleshy leaves are somewhat fattish and round or kidney shaped. They have a pronounced indent where the petiole meets the leaf. Grow in clusters of low-lying

FORAGER NOTE: Mountain sorrel is distinguished from the docks and sheep sorrel by its rounded or kidney-shaped leaves.

leaves with erect protruding flower stalks. Flowers grow in dense clusters along the stalk and are green or reddish, becoming darker red as they become winged achenes, or seedpods.

Range and Habitat

Western United States from Alaska and the Northwest Territories to California and Texas. Common in the higher mountains of the West. Found in alpine, subalpine, arctic, and tundra zones, especially nestled in rocks; most often in moist areas near streams or melting snowpack.

Comments

Leaves, stems, and seeds are edible raw or cooked. Tart-flavored leaves can be used like rhubarb or to make a lemonade-like drink. Eat leaves and stems raw, cooked, or pickled as you would any versatile leafy green vegetable.

RECIPE

Alpine Sorrel Fruit Salad

Harvest 1 cup alpine sorrel leaves. Wash and pat dry with a clean dish towel. Cut leaves in half, then cut in half again. Slice 4 bananas into ¼" rounds. Slice ⅔ cup dried apricots in half, then half again. Combine all ingredients in a bowl, and toss to combine. Top with a pinch or two of fresh-ground nutmeg.

Variation: Use fresh apricots. Squeeze juice of 1 fresh lime over fruit mixture.

SHEEP SORREL
Rumex acetosella

Family: Polygonaceae
Other names: Common sheep sorrel, red sorrel, sour weed, field sorrel, spinach dock, garden sorrel, *Acetosella vulgaris*
Lookalikes: Mountain sorrel, the docks
WARNING: See oxalates discussion in introduction.

Description
This nonnative perennial is a *Rumex* like the docks, and the erect flower stalk that gives way to rust-colored achenes is similar to that of the much larger, sturdier docks. It is difficult to see the difference in photos, but sheep sorrel is much smaller and tenderer than the docks.

Stems are very slender but erect, 4"–24" tall. Whale-shaped leaves are less than an inch to 6" long and less than 1" wide.

Sheep sorrel has a characteristic simple (not compound) leaf shape that

FORAGER NOTE: Much smaller than the docks. The leaves remain tender even after the plant has gone to seed.

resembles a whale with wings, or fins, at the leaf base. Not all leaves, even on the same plant, will have these curlicues, but when they do they are about one-quarter the size of the leaf or smaller. Leaves are otherwise oval or widely lanceolate

Inflorescences are whorled flower spikes arranged in a narrow pillar along the stalk. Flowers are maroon, red, or light green in color. Fruits are achenes (small seed-like structures) and are rust colored. The herbaceous perennial blooms June to August.

Reproduces by seed and by creeping rhizomatous roots about 8"–2' (some reports say 5') underground.

Range and Habitat

Naturalized from Eurasia, sheep sorrel is now considered a noxious weed in about half of the US states. Grows from Alaska to Texas and across the United States with the possible exception of the deep south. Sheep sorrel colonizes acidic and low-nitrogen (poor) soils, grass fields, pastures, disturbed sites, clear-cuts, and recent burn areas from about 4,000'–11,200' (lower in the northern areas) in elevation throughout the Rockies. Grows in moist, riparian areas, on dry open slopes, and along roadsides. Shade tolerant, it is also found in forests. Found all the way down to sea level in other parts of the country. Hardy to USDA Zone 3.

RECIPE

Trail Recipe

Pack a blackened tofu or roast beef sandwich, and add a big pile of sheep sorrel leaves that you find along the way. You'll love me for this one.

Comments

The first time I discovered sheep sorrel, I felt like I had discovered some old French culinary delicacy. It was delightful. The fact that sheep sorrel is classified as a noxious weed in twenty-three states (which means herbicide city—more poisons please) is mind-boggling. This is one of the loveliest wild edible greens I know of. Its taste is fresh, light, and with a unique lemony punch. The texture is so smooth it melts in your mouth. Sheep sorrel eradication efforts could be a great opportunity for foragers to start working with local governments and farmers. Offer to harvest this wonderful crop and save them the time and money of buying and applying more herbicides.

The leaves, roots, flowers (raw or cooked), and seeds (ground into flour) are edible. Leaves can be used as a curdling agent for milk products.

Sheep sorrel has a long history of cultivation around the world. It has been used in traditional recipes in Russia, the Ukraine, Lithuania, Hungary, Turkey, Poland, Bulgaria, Nigeria, Greece, and other countries.

RECIPE

Polish Sorrel Soup

Cook 4 eggs in boiling water for 8 minutes until hard boiled. Cool by soaking in cold water, peel, and set aside. Cook 4 medium-size potatoes cut into quarters in boiling water until tender, about 15 minutes. Drain and set aside.

Bring 6 cups chicken or vegetable broth (homemade or bouillon) to a boil; reduce to a simmer. Add 1 cup chopped sorrel leaves, and return to a simmer.

In a separate bowl mix 3 tablespoons organic white flour with 12 ounces sour cream; stir into broth. Add salt if desired.

Divide cooked, quartered potatoes among four soup bowls. Place 1 hard-boiled egg, cut into quarters, into each bowl. Pour soup into prepared bowls. Serve hot.

Variation: Leave out the sour cream but still add the flour. In this case, sauté the flour in organic canola oil for 2 minutes on medium to low heat, stirring constantly. Then add it to the broth and stir in. The soup will appear creamy but without the dairy.

CURLY DOCK
Rumex crispus

Family: Polygonaceae

Other names: Narrowleaf dock, sour dock, yellow dock (because the root is yellow), crispy dock, dockweed

Related species: Willow dock (*R. salicifolius* or *R. triangulivalvis*), western dock (*R. aquaticus* or *R. occidentalis*), broadleaf dock (*R. obtusi-folius*), canaigre dock (*R. hymenosepalus*), pale dock (*R. altisimus*)

WARNING: Contains oxalic acid and so should be eaten as part of a diverse diet. See oxalates discussion in introduction.

FORAGER NOTE: Even though the flowers are green, it is more common to see the burnt-red seedpods standing erect along roadsides.

Description

Docks, perennial Eurasian implants, have low basal leaf clusters that grow to about 1' across. Erect, sometimes branched clusters of flower stalks stick straight up. Flowers are without petals. They are light green or greenish red, growing in tight, erect, whorled clusters. The flowers give way to burnt-red or dark brown clusters of smooth, three-sided achenes with a large seed lump visible, often lighter colored, in the center. Inflorescences are about 6"–18" long.

Curly dock grows 1'–5' tall. Stalks are round, hairless, and ridged. It is notable by it large single, curly, wavy, or undulating leaf margins, hence the name. Leaves are entire, lanceolate, and hairless. Basal leaves are the largest. Leaves are smaller, with shorter petioles along the stalk. The light green or purplish midrib is pronounced. The root of the curly dock is yellow.

Curly dock is distinguished from golden dock by its seedpods. Golden dock seedpods are serrated and have long needle-like points sticking out. It also has leaves coming out from between the seed heads, whereas curly dock leaves do not.

Range and Habitat

Commonly found throughout the plains and foothills regions, especially in ditches and disturbed ground from Alaska to Texas. Curly dock and golden dock are the only docks found in Colorado.

Docks are seen commonly along roads, ditches, waste places, and gravely roadsides throughout the region. The erect burnt-red (sometimes yellow or light green) flower or seed heads are easily visible as you drive by.

Comments

Leaves, young flower stalks, and petioles are edible raw or cooked. Seeds are also edible but bitter. Leaves are most tender and least bitter when young. Stalk can be peeled to reveal the sweeter inside portion. The leaves taste somewhat like kale with a note of sour. They lose their toughness when cooked. Leaves are good simmered in soup stock or stew.

Roots and young leaves are used medicinally for liver issues.

Seeds can be used as flour, to make piecrust and crackers, or to flavor vinegar. They must be rubbed to release the buckwheat-shaped, three-sided seed from its casing. Seeds are rich in iron but bitter. Some reports say leaching improves taste.

The *Rumex* genus consists of about 200 species, including docks and sorrels. In photos dock and sorrel look very similar, but in real life it is fairly easy to tell them apart. Docks are much bigger, with tougher leaves. Dock leaves themselves, however, can vary quite a bit. Dock species are known to hybridize with one another, making it somewhat difficult to distinguish between specific species. All are edible in the same ways, so it is not essential to identify the specific species.

RECIPE

Dock Leaf Nachos

Start with a stack of 6 fresh organic corn tortillas. Heat 2 tablespoons canola oil in a large skillet to medium-high heat. Cook tortillas in pan until they just begin to harden, one side then the next. Remove tortillas from pan and crack into several small pieces. Place chips into a glass pie dish.

Preheat oven to broil.

Evenly spread 1 cup black or pinto beans across the top of the chips. Add 1 cup finely chopped young dock leaves and 3 tablespoons chopped onion. Add ½ cup chopped green pepper and 1 cup cheddar or mozzarella cheese or cheese substitute. Top with chopped jalapeño (optional).

Place in oven on second to highest rack in center of broiler coil. Rotate after 2 minutes. Cook until cheese is bubbling and just begins to brown. Remove from oven and serve as is or with fresh salsa.

Variation: Use pre-made corn chips. Boil dock leaves first for 7 minutes; drain and add to nachos as described above.

RECIPE

Stuffed Zucchini with Dock

Summer is almost synonymous with creative zucchini recipes. Here's one of my favorites, and it is amenable to endless variation. This looks like a long, complicated recipe but is actually easy. Basically you just need to precook the zucchini canoes, sautéing some veggies and shrimp in the meantime. Combine them, add cheese, and bake.

First cook 1 cup brown rice. Leftover rice works great too.

Preheat oven to 350°F. Slice 2 large zucchinis in half, and scoop out the seeds; retain the pulp. This leaves canoe-shaped zucchini halves. Lightly coat the bottom of a glass baking dish with olive or coconut oil. Use a dish big enough to fit the 4 zucchini canoes. Place canoes in baking dish skin side down, and bake for 30 to 40 minutes.

Take ½ cup young dock leaves and ½ cup young flower stalks. Wash and pat dry. Chop leaves and chop flower stalks into very small pieces, as small as possible. Set aside.

Chop the following into very small pieces and keep in separate piles on cutting board: retained zucchini pulp, ¼ cup green onions (OK to use chives or onion instead), 2 carrots, and 8 shrimp.

While zucchini is baking, in a large skillet heat 1 tablespoon olive oil to medium-high heat. Add the green onions; sauté for 4 minutes. Add the carrots; sauté 4 more minutes. Add the shrimp, toss to combine, and cook 4 more minutes. Add the rest of the veggies, 1 cup cooked rice, and a splash of Bragg Liquid Aminos. Add ¼ teaspoon crushed hot peppers. Sauté for about 8 minutes over medium heat, stirring to prevent sticking. Remove from heat and place in a bowl to cool. Once mixture is cooled, add 1 egg and mix in well.

When zucchini canoes are done, remove from oven. Fill to heaping with the rice and dock mixture. Top with grated cheese or cheese substitute. Sprinkle on some paprika. Bake for 15 to 20 minutes, or until cheese is melted and just begins to bubble and brown.

WILD LICORICE
Glycyrrhiza lepidota

Family: Fabaceae

Other names: American licorice, sweet root

Lookalikes: Several species of sweet vetches (*Hedysarum* spp., which are also called licorice root); clovers, alfalfa, St. John's wort, Jacob's ladder, milk vetch (*Astragalus* spp.), and golden banner (**poisonous**)

WARNING: Do not ingest if you're pregnant or taking steroid therapy. Some sources warn that large amounts can be toxic and should be avoided by those suffering from liver disease, glaucoma, high blood pressure, or heart disease.

Description

This aromatic native perennial can reach more than 3' high but on average is closer to 2' tall. It has taproots that can reach 3'–4' down and spreading rhizomatous root systems.

Leaves are pinnately divided and consist of organized rows of eleven to nineteen small, lance-shaped, opposite leaflets, each about ¾"–1½" long. There is always an odd number of leaflets, with a single one at the very tip of each leaf stem. Leaves can be a bit sticky. The leaf stem is often in a sweeping downward arch.

Flowers are similar to those of white clover (*Trifolium repens*), but the cluster is more elongated than the rounder clover flower head. Pea-like flowers are white, yellowish, or greenish-white (sometimes purplish). Flowers grow from leafless stems that originate at the axils (corners) between the leaf stem and stalk.

Brownish spiny, burred seedpods are unique to this species within the Pea family.

Range and Habitat

From about the Mississippi River westward to California and Texas and north to British Columbia. Moist fields, ditches, meadows, slow-moving streams, and other moist areas in the plains and foothills.

Comments

Leaves, young shoots, and roots are edible. All parts can be eaten raw or cooked.

Roots are sweet and often likened to sweet potatoes. Can be pounded to remove fibers before eating. Taproots are used for a variety of medicinal purposes. Taproots can be carefully dug out of the ground and dried in the sun. Harvest roots in the fall with a shovel. Roots can be 3'–4' deep. Roots also make a good tea.

Related to the commercial licorice variety (*G. glabra*).

RECIPE

Roasted Wild Licorice Root

Build a small fire in a safe area away from brush, shrubs, and low-hanging tree branches. Allow a large pile of coals to form. If you have a fire grate for grilling, place that over the fire and allow fire to burn down into coals.

Place roots on the grilling grate. As each side just begins to brown, rotate and continue rotating numerous times for about 1 hour (depending on how hot the coals are). When the roots are soft but not burned, remove from heat and enjoy.

Variations: Cut in half and sprinkle wild flax seeds or evening primrose seeds on top. You can also bake the roots in the oven as you would a baked potato.

ALFALFA
Medicago sativa

Family: Fabaceae
Other names: Lucerne
Lookalikes: Yellow and white sweet clover (before they bloom)
WARNING: Can be problematic for people with lupus and gout. Contains saponin, which in large quantities can cause problems. Avoid during pregnancy and while breastfeeding. The sprouts manufacture a substance called canavanine to protect them from predation. This substance is toxic to humans and can sometimes cause lupus- or arthritis-like symptoms. Small portions are probably safe for healthy adults, but monitoring for joint stiffness is recommended.

Description

This long-living, nonnative perennial is erect and gangly. The plant's height depends on the growing conditions but usually matures at about 2'–3' tall. Stalk is branched and generally smooth.

Alfalfa leaves are formed in clusters of three small oblong leaflets similar to those of clovers, but the leaflets are somewhat more narrow and elongated (ovular). Leaves are alternate along the stalk and not spaced uniformly. The upper half of the leaflets are sharply toothed. There is a noticeable darker indent and a slight fold at the vein, down the middle of each leaf.

The pea-like flowers form ovular rounded clusters of purple or bluish, rose, sometimes yellowish or whitish flowers that are up to about ⅜" long. Forms seedpods much like other members of the legume family but curled like a ram's horn. Seeds are small and kidney shaped. The plant has a very robust root system.

Range and Habitat

Grows in disturbed areas and pastures. In our region it is most common in the foothills and mountains from 3,000'–9,000' in elevation. Typically grows in fairly nutrient rich soil, which helps it accumulate so many nutrients.

Comments

Flowers, leaves, and young shoots can be eaten raw, cooked, or dried. Generally harvest only the upper half of the plant. Also, grazing of alfalfa makes it more bitter, so ungrazed plants are best. The seeds can be eaten sprouted, roasted, or made into flour.

RECIPE

Dried Alfalfa Supplement

Harvest flowers and leaves from top half of plant by stripping them off the stalk. Dry on trays, in bags, or by hanging in a dark place with good airflow. Once fully dried, place in an airtight jar. After a few days, open the jar, shake the contents, and reseal. If the moisture has redistributed itself and the plant does not seem fully dry, leave lid off for 6–12 hours and then reseal. Repeat every day until flowers are fully dried.

Can be stored whole or crushed into a powder. When ready to use, add to soups, stews, sauces, or smoothies for a nutritional boost.

Can also be used to make tea. Boil water and steep dried alfalfa greens for 5 to 10 minutes. Add honey and a 1 teaspoon fresh ginger root if desired.

Alfalfa is an important food crop for both humans and animals. It is used as feed for poultry, livestock, and in the wild is grazed upon by deer, elk, antelopes, geese, grouse, sandhill cranes, mallard ducks, partridges, pheasants, and others. The leaves are also used commercially to fortify human baby food and as dietary supplements.

This naturalized Eurasian implant is also a pollen source for bees. It is high in vitamins A, B, C, E, K, and P, as well as calcium, potassium, iron, and protein.

It has been reported that alfalfa was brought to this country to increase yields of milk in dairy cows. In *Medicinal Plants of the Mountain West,* Michael Moore points out that because of modern agricultural practices, commercial varieties of alfalfa no longer accumulate as many nutrients, so its reputation as a milk increaser has diminished. He claims that wild varieties are still exceptionally nutritious.

A genetically modified alfalfa has been grown in the United States. Because of concerns about safety and cross-contamination, it has been embroiled in legal battles for several years.

Alfalfa is a nitrogen fixer and so a great addition to a home garden. It often will find its way to your garden all on its own.

RECIPE

French Lentils and Alfalfa Flower Heads

French lentils are a gorgeous smoky green or gray color and combined with the striking purple alfalfa flowers make a deeply stunning dish. Set your table to highlight these natural colors, or add a pop of complementary color with bright flowers or colorful cloth napkins.

Rinse 1 cup lentils in lukewarm or cool water until no foam appears. In a soup pot, bring the lentils and 4 cups water to a high simmer. Reduce immediately to a very low simmer. Cook uncovered for 20 to 30 minutes until lentils are soft. Make sure there is enough water that the lentils remain covered throughout the cooking time. If water becomes too low, add more. Do not allow to boil, as this will produce soggy, waterlogged lentils rather than distinct, firm ones.

Place ⅓ cup alfalfa flower heads into a medium-size bowl. When lentils are done cooking, drain water and immediately pour hot lentils over the flower heads. Allow the hot lentils to sit on top of the flower heads for a few minutes. Meanwhile add ¼ cup raw chopped chives or wild onion, ¼ teaspoon salt, ¼ teaspoon pepper, and 1 teaspoon olive oil or butter. Mix gently so that you don't crush the flower heads. Serve warm.

SWEET CLOVER
Melilotus officinalis

Family: Fabaceae
Other names: Common sweet clover, yellow sweet clover, white sweet clover, sweetclover, melilot, *M. albus*
Lookalikes: Alfalfa, all clovers, golden banner (poisonous)
WARNING: Never eat moldy plants. Leaves, especially if poorly dried or moldy, can cause thinning of the blood. Leaves contain coumarin and dicoumarol, which can cause uncontrolled internal bleeding. **Deadly.**

Do not confuse with golden banner, which is poisonous.

> RECIPE
>
> **Sweet Clover Tea**
>
> Snip off enough flower stalks and leaves to fill your tea steeper. Boil water and then allow to cool for a few minutes. Pour over plant pieces, and steep for 3 to 10 minutes. Add honey if desired. On the trail you can make sun tea by placing the ingredients in your water bottle and allowing the sun to do the rest as you hike along.

Description

This sweetly pungent, very common annual, biennial, or perennial grows 1'–6' tall in disturbed areas. It's three-leaved like other clovers but taller. Alternate leaves are oblong or elliptic. Before it flowers, sweet clover looks just like alfalfa, although the flowers are quite different.

Yellow or white flowers are small and pea-like. Individual plants are either yellow or white flowered. Each flower is about ¼" long, forming into elongated, slender clusters or long, narrow spikes along branches, which branch off the tall main stalk. Blooms early summer to fall. Very strong taproot is impossible to pull out of the ground by hand.

Range and Habitat

This plant is a widespread invasive weed and often significantly hampers native species growth. It thrives in dry conditions but grows even bigger along stream-beds. Harvest freely in such situations.

Grilled Chicken with Yellow Sweet Clover Garnish

Marinate 2 chicken breasts in enough olive oil to coat them, ½ teaspoon salt, and ½ teaspoon pepper for 1 or more hours. Grill one side over medium heat for 5–10 minutes, then flip. Grill the other side for about 5–10 minutes until the chicken is no longer pink in the middle. Place on bed of lettuce and garnish with 2 teaspoons yellow sweet clover flowers.

Comments

Flowers, shoots, and leaves are tender and edible raw or cooked. Some accounts say cooked roots are edible.

Use flowers fresh or dried for tea. There is conflicting information about whether to use dried leaves. Some sources say they can cause bleeding. I suspect this is from improper drying methods that cause mold to accumulate, but I do not know this for sure. Other sources say dried leaves are edible and can be used to flavor pastry and soups.

Use young leaves cooked or raw as you would any green. Shoots can be cooked like asparagus.

Strong pleasant tasting and somewhat vanilla flavored. Flowers are used to flavor gruyère cheese and can be dried and used as flavoring for soups.

In wetter years, cattle have been known to die from foraging on sweet clover because of dicoumarol production, which prevents blood from clotting. This can also cause humans to bleed to death even from minor wounds. This is said to have led to the invention of rat poison. Sweet clover adds nitrogen to the soil and provides excellent nectar for bees.

RED CLOVER
Trifolium pratense

Family: Fabaceae
Lookalikes: White clover, alsike clover, alfalfa, golden banner
WARNING: There are many **toxic members** of the Pea family. Make sure you positively identify this species before ingesting.

Description
This nonnative biennial or perennial has tiny, slender pea-like flowers that form dense balls at the top of thin stalks. The inflorescences are reddish, pink, or dark pink and often have a lighter-colored base.

Red clover grows from about 6"–30" tall. The stalks are hollow, erect, and often somewhat sprawling. Leaves and stalk are hairy. Leaves are trifoliate, divided into three leaflets. The leaves are ½"–1" long and alternate. They are green with a pale green or whitish V-shaped marking (chevron). The white marking distinguishes red clover from alsike clover, which has only green leaves. Four to six branches per stem.

Range and Habitat

Red clover is a Eurasian immigrant that is now found widely across the United States. Especially likes disturbed ground and full sun. Will grow larger in moist areas. Found to 8,500' elevation or higher.

Comments

This is the family of legumes, peas, and beans. Like them, clovers are nitrogen fixers and therefore splendid at improving poor soil—good for your garden and good for you.

RECIPE

Fresh Clover Salad

Combine a handful of lettuce, a handful of arugula leaves, and a handful of clover (flowers and leaves). Toss together in a large bowl.

In a separate small bowl prepare the dressing. Combine 1 teaspoon olive oil, 1 teaspoon sweet rice vinegar, 1 teaspoon tahini, and a splash of soy sauce. Add 1 tablespoon chopped green onions. Mix well until oils and liquids are combined. Let sit for 5 minutes or longer. Pour over salad; toss well.

I was at the Colorado Permaculture Guild's 2012 Annual Convergence, which was held at the 63rd Street Farm in Boulder, Colorado. I began an impromptu wild edible walk with one of the participants. We came upon a huge patch of red clover, and my new friend was totally in love with it. She told me that her family regularly buys red clover for medicinal tea. She had never realized how easy it was to find it growing wild. I mention this because so many of us buy food and medicine from stores and have no idea what it looks like in the wild, how it grows, or how easy it is to go out and find these special herbs ourselves.

RECIPE

Red Clover Tea

Use a teapot with a fitted steeper. Combine in the steeper 5 red clover flowers, 4 sprigs lemon balm from your garden, and half that amount of fennel leaves or root. When water boils, pour over herbs and allow to steep about 8 minutes. Add honey and stir in. Serve hot or cold.

Variation: Add 1 clove garlic, fresh sliced ginger, or a pinch of turmeric.

RECIPE

Sautéed Clover Flowers with Candied Pecans

Harvest 1 cup flower heads of red clover. Rinse dirt off and set aside. In a heavy skillet heat 1 tablespoon coconut oil to medium. Toss in ½ cup raw, unsalted pecans. Toss continuously until they start to smell roasted. Just as they begin to smell good and turn brown, decrease heat to very low. Drizzle 1 tablespoon honey over them. Add a pinch of salt. Toss for a minute or two until honey coats the nuts. Remove from heat, and pour into a bowl.

Using the same skillet (unless you have burned the honey), bring 1 teaspoon olive oil or butter to medium-high heat. Add the clover flowers. Toss gently and sauté for 4 minutes. Add 2 cups chopped spinach; toss together and sauté 4 more minutes. Remove from heat and top with the candied pecans. Serve warm or at room temperature.

WHITE CLOVER
Trifolium repens

Family: Fabaceae

Other names: Dutch clover

WARNING: There are many **toxic members** of the Pea family. Make sure you positively identify this species before ingesting.

Description

White clover is low growing, 4"–10" high. Its small pea-like flowers form a loose ball, sometimes with a pink tinge. These flower tufts are about ½" wide. Leaves are trifoliate (three-lobed), sometimes with a pale green or whitish V-shaped marking.

> FORAGER NOTE: Sometimes leaves are marked with white chevrons, sometimes not. Look closely at the individual flowers, looking for tiny purple spots and green teeth.

The species name *repens* means "creeping" in Latin, and true to its name, white clover creeps along the ground planting itself in the soil (much like strawberry shoots) at its joints.

Range and Habitat

A Eurasian immigrant that is now found widely across the United States. Especially likes disturbed ground; cool, moist areas; and full sun up to timber line.

RECIPE

Peach and Clover Salad

Peach season on the western slope is short and very sweet. For an unusual local salad that is just as good for dessert as it is for an appetizer, harvest 1 cup clover flowers. Rinse if necessary. Slice 4 fresh peaches into smaller than bite-size chunks. Combine in a bowl with the clover flowers. Add 2 tablespoons champagne vinaigrette; toss gently. Garnish with fresh sprigs of mint.

Variation: Slice about 2 cups seedless red grapes in half, and add to mixture.

Comments

Flowers, stalks, leaves, and seeds can be eaten cooked, dried, or raw. White clovers are widespread and common; they make a great trail snack or fresh addition to a meal while camping.

Some people find that eating too many raw clovers causes bloating. To improve digestibility, clovers can be boiled with a bit of salt.

White clovers, like other clovers, are often found as garden and lawn volunteers (weeds). Clovers are a perfect example of how to turn weeding your garden into a fruitful and nutritious harvest.

Clovers add nitrogen to the soil and provide food for bees, other pollinators, and cattle. High in protein, they are a good forage crop for livestock.

Make a great addition to tea and salads. Wine can also be made from clover flowers.

RECIPE

Dried Clover and Rice Breakfast

Harvest white clover flower heads after they have gone to seed. Lay out on a tray and allow to dry in a dark room. Store in a sealed glass jar until ready to use.

Prepare short-grain brown rice according to rice's cooking instructions. When rice is almost finished cooking, prepare 1 fried egg. Heat skillet to medium high. Add butter or oil, and fry egg to your liking.

Fill bowl two-thirds full with warm rice. Place the egg on top. Sprinkle crushed dried clover seeds and flower heads on top, about ½ teaspoon. Sprinkle with Braggs or soy sauce and a bit of olive or flax oil. Add a sprinkle of hot pepper flakes if desired.

LAMB'S-QUARTER
Chenopodium album

Family: Chenopodiaceae

Other names: Wild spinach, goosefoot, white goosefoot, wild quinoa

Lookalikes: Strawberry blite, hairy nightshade (*Solanum physalifolium*), ground cherry nightshade (*Solanum villosum*). Both nightshades may be at least somewhat toxic, often varying from plant to plant from safe to very toxic.

WARNING: See oxalates discussion in introduction. Seeds and seedpods should be rinsed to remove saponin.

Description
This annual herb has toothed, rounded-triangular or goosefoot-shaped leaves that are arranged alternately along gently ridged, erect, often-branched stems.

From above they appear whorled. Leaves are soft and fleshy and, especially when young, have a whitish crystalline residue emanating from the leaf base. Leaves hang from slightly drooping petioles and are ½"–3" long.

This fast-growing annual ranges from a few inches to 4'–5' tall (sometimes up to 6½'), depending on soil and moisture conditions.

Flowers are small, pale green, and round, with no petals.

As the days shorten or water becomes scarce, lamb's-quarter begins to set seed. First, tight buds form along the tops of branches. In early fall you will begin to see seeds popping out of the seed capsules. Seeds are flat, mostly black but also brown or reddish, and about 1 millimeter across, or about one-fourth the size of commercial quinoa seeds.

Range and Habitat

A prolific pioneer species that colonizes disturbed areas and grows well in all soil types all over the world. In the Rocky Mountains it grows up to 11,000' in elevation or higher.

Comments

Leaves, stalks, and flowers are edible raw or cooked. Seeds are also edible sprouted or cooked. Seeds must be thrashed and winnowed and can be eaten cooked or sprouted.

In *Edible Wild Plants: Wild Foods from Dirt to Plate,* John Kallas calls lamb's-quarter wild spinach in order to "give this plant the food-related name recognition it deserves." I couldn't agree more; it's a delicious and prolific wild edible pioneer.

This very common weed is an excellent source of food. Lamb's-quarter, along with dandelions, should help us all transform our negative weeding mind-set into a happily abundant harvesting mind-set. For some reason our conquer-and-control culture despises plants that voluntarily join our garden ecosystems. These volunteers are not our enemies, and if we can relax a bit and learn to appreciate and be nurtured and nourished by them, life becomes a bit easier. Wild edibles are our caretakers, and wild spinach is a prolific one.

RECIPE

Crisp Tofu Squares

Cut 1 block firm tofu into ½"–1" squares. Heat 3 tablespoons canola oil in saucepan until it sizzles when you throw a drop of water onto it. Fry tofu squares until crisp on all sides, tossing gently as they cook.

Its big fluffy leaves provide tender, delicious greens from early spring on. They can be eaten raw or cooked. They can also be dried to a green powder and added to smoothies throughout the winter. Their production tapers off in the heat of summer, but some young plants will reappear by fall. Because lamb's-quarter reseeds so readily, you may want to tame the stands in your garden. Harvest or com-

post seeds to prevent an all-out takeover, but I highly recommend leaving a good stand for food. Remember, this is an annual, so there is no need, except for aesthetic reasons, to pull young plants out when weeding. You can if you want, but the real control strategy if you are trying to reduce the lamb's-quarter in your yard is to harvest the seeds in late summer or early fall, before they escape and replant themselves.

Seeds are time-consuming to winnow after harvest. The green capsule should be removed. It contains saponin and is bitter. The capsules can be toasted and then the seeds crushed out and winnowed, or you can just let them dry out and then crush and winnow the seeds. Winnowing works best when there is a smooth, steady breeze.

RECIPE

Wild Spinach Salad

Harvest leaves before the plant flowers. Large and small leaves are good. Mix with other early lettuce greens and baby chard.

To make dressing, in a separate bowl combine 1 tablespoon olive oil, 1 teaspoon balsamic vinegar, 1 heaping teaspoon tahini, 1 clove fresh garlic, chopped, sea salt, and fresh-ground pepper to taste. Mix well with a tiny eggbeater until well combined. Pour over salad; toss until all greens are covered. Top with Crisp Tofu Squares (see recipe above) and 1 teaspoon flax seeds.

STRAWBERRY BLITE
Chenopodium capitatum

Family: Chenopodiaceae
Other names: Beetroot, strawberry spinach, Indian-paint, Indian ink, blite goosefoot
Lookalikes: Lamb's-quarter
WARNING: Leaves contain oxalates, as does spinach (see oxalates discussion in introduction). Seeds may be toxic in large amounts. Also contains saponin, which can be toxic. People with a tendency to rheumatism, arthritis, gout, kidney stones, or hyperacidity should take special caution if including this plant in their diet, since it can aggravate their condition.

Description
This annual member of the Goosefoot family is erect, sometimes decumbent (lying down but with branches sticking a upward), growing to about 2' tall; in poor conditions much smaller,

about 6" high. Varies in size dramatically, much like its relative lamb's-quarter. Size is dependent on growing conditions.

Strawberry blite is notable by its bulbous light green flowers that cluster along the stalk and become weird looking, bulbous bright red fleshy fruits. They somewhat resemble strawberries but grow clustered along the stalk and are about ¾" wide (sometimes much tinier).

Leaves are alternate, from very small to about 3" long. They are broad and triangular, with wavy margins or deeply lobed, bluntly pointed teeth. Leaves resemble those of lamb's-quarter.

RECIPE

Blite Salad

Harvest 1 cup strawberry blite greens. Wash and spin in a salad spinner. Combine in a large salad bowl with 3 cups fluffy, lighter salad greens, such as red curly lettuce. Add 1 cup watercress.

Chop all greens to bite-size pieces. Toss well with 1 tablespoon olive oil, ½ tablespoon fresh-squeezed lemon juice, ½ teaspoon apple cider vinegar, and salt and pepper to taste. Add the red fruits of strawberry blite and 2 tablespoon crushed cashews. Enjoy this fresh, crunchy, sweet, spicy, and fruity salad.

Variation: Substitute slivered almonds for cashews.

Range and Habitat

From Alaska south through New Mexico. Also found in the northern states and eastward across Canada. Prefers moist soil and sun, though I have seen it growing in partial shade and in dry soil.

Comments

Leaves and fruits are edible raw or cooked. Leaves can be used like lamb's-quarter.

The first time strawberry blite appeared in my yard, I had absolutely no idea what it was. As the name suggests, it looks like a bulbously bright red disease taking over an otherwise vibrant plant.

I've read accounts of this species that say the fruits are bland and the seeds problematic. I totally don't find this to be the case. I think these fruits are sweet, soft, and delicious. There are probably variations within the species, but I have found that the seeds are easily chewed, much like raspberry seeds, just adding a little texture. I would actually rate this up there with thimbleberry as one of the most delicious yet least-known wild fruits, with the added awesomeness that the plant also provides tender greens. The only problem is that it's not very common and does not reseed readily, so harvest thoughtfully.

GIANT HYSSOPS
Agastache spp.

Family: Lamiaceae
Related species: Blue hyssop/anise hyssop/lavender hyssop/licorice mint (*A. foeniculum*); giant hyssop/nettle-leaf giant hyssop/horse mint (*A. urticifolia*)
Lookalikes: Mint, stinging nettle, catnip

Description

This strong-smelling perennial subshrub looks like really huge mint but without the mint smell. Flowers cluster at the tops of stalks. *Agastache* has a very pungent, distinct, but not minty smell.

Blue/Anise hyssop *(A. foeniculum):* Blue or lavender flowers with erect, sometimes branched stalks that reach 1'–4' in height. Inflorescences are clusters of small trumpet-shaped flowers, together forming a cluster about 8" long at top of stalk. Coarsely toothed, opposite leaves, darker on top. Smells like licorice or anise.

Giant hyssop *(A. urticifolia):* Pinkish, whitish, or lavender flowers bloom in late spring. Slowly spreads by rhizomatous roots. Stalks are single or branched and grow up to 3'–6' tall. Flowers are trumpet shaped with long protruding stamens and stigmas. They form in a tubular, gently pointed cluster along the top portion of the stalk 1'–6' long. From afar, appears somewhat like a clover head but elongated. Simple, pointed ovate (or widely lance-shaped) leaves are

---

RECIPE

Cold *Agastache* Gazpacho

Excellent in late summer when tomatoes are farm fresh and ripe.

In a food processor combine 6 large tomatoes and about 9 large hyssop leaves. Add hot or sweet peppers, such as ½ roasted Thai pepper and ½ roasted Serrano pepper, although any peppers can be used. (To prepare peppers, roast on grill or in toaster oven until skin is browned. Allow to cool. Peel and remove seeds.) A roasted green bell pepper works well too.

Add a splash of sherry vinegar, a splash of olive oil, and a splash of soy sauce or a dash of salt. Add a scant teaspoon of honey. Pulse until combined and well chopped but not totally liquefied and uniform.

Serve room temperature or chilled. Garnish with fresh or dried parsley leaves and chopped chives or red onion.

opposite, toothed, and widely spaced along the stalk. They are darker on the upper surface, lighter underneath.

Range and Habitat
A. foeniculum is found along the West Coast, comes into the Rockies, and is spotty in Colorado. It is relegated to the West, from British Columbia to California and some parts of Colorado, but not New Mexico and Arizona. Favors meadows, foothills, creekbanks, and roadsides.

A. urticifolia is found across the northern part of the country and from the Northwest Territories to western Colorado.

Comments
Seeds, leaves, and flowers can be eaten raw or cooked. The seeds of blue hyssop (also called anise hyssop) are best and can be used as a flavoring like anise or licorice seeds. Seeds can be used in sweet or savory dishes and added to jam or preserves. The anise-scented leaves are somewhat sweet tasting and can be used as tea and in potpourri. Nettle-leaf giant hyssop can be used in the same ways, but it does not impart the licorice-like flavor.

Well liked by bees, hummingbirds, and butterflies.

RECIPE

Stewed Anise Plums and Peaches

Harvest 1 cup fresh flowers of the anise hyssop. Heat 6 cups water to a boil. Pour over the flowers, and let steep for about 8 hours.

Optional: Add ¼ cup brandy. If desired, sweeten with 1–3 teaspoons honey or sugar. Add ¼ teaspoon cinnamon, and ⅛ teaspoon nutmeg. Add a dash of vanilla, and stir ingredients together.

Cut 3 fresh peaches and 3 plums in half and remove the pits. Place fruit halves flat side down in a saucepan that is large enough that the fruit is snuggled together but not crushed. Pour the tea mixture over the fruit.

Bring to a low simmer over low heat. Now and again make sure that fruit is not sticking to the bottom of the pan by scraping under fruit with a spatula. If sticking, reduce heat. Simmer, covered, until liquid has mostly evaporated and has become thicker. Serve alone, over ice cream, or with a dollop of sweetened ricotta cheese. (Mix some sugar into the ricotta, and blend well.)

MINT
Mentha spp.

Family: Lamiaceae
Other names: Wild mint, field mint, poleo mint. Field mint (*M. arvensis*) is a common species in our area.
Lookalikes: Stinging nettle, giant hyssop
WARNING: Some people are allergic to mint.

RECIPE

Fresh Mint Sorbet

In a saucepan heat 6 cups water just to a simmer. Add 1½ cups packed, finely chopped mint leaves. Stir and simmer for about 20 minutes. Remove from heat and add ¾ cup honey. Stir until dissolved. Place in refrigerator until fully cold.

Pour into prechilled ice-cream maker according to manufacturer's directions. Serve with a fresh sprig of mint.

Variation: Top with shavings of dark chocolate and a few drippings of honey.

Description

In my experience, if it smells like mint and has a square stem, it is mint.

Wild mints are perennial, and many species are native. There are several species of wild mints, and they can smell like peppermint, spearmint, or some combination. Leaves vary but are basically ovate, mildly to very pointed, and toothed. Leaves are close to the main stalk and more or less horizontal to the ground. Leaves are spaced in opposite pairs along the branches and main stem.

RECIPE

Fruit Salad with Fresh Mint

Combine whatever fresh fruits are in season in a large bowl. Some to consider are peaches, plums, watermelon, and cantaloupe. Cut into bite-size pieces, 1 to 3 cups of each fruit.

Wash and pat dry ¼ to ½ cup mint, depending on how much fruit you are using. Chop roughly. Add to fruit mixture; toss to combine. Add fresh-squeezed lime or lemon juice if desired.

Serve immediately, or refrigerate overnight and serve cold.

Rounded purple or lavender flower clusters grow either at the top of the stalk or in whorls along the stems at the corners where the leaves or petioles meet the stalk, depending on the species. Grows 6"–3' high.

Range and Habitat

Moderate to low elevations from Alaska to Florida. Especially in moist areas like banks of beaver ponds, fields, streambanks, and open meadows, but once established it is widely tolerant of variations. Plains, foothills, meadows. Part shade or sun.

Comments

There are several species of wild mints. Flavor varies, but all can be used interchangeably. Eat raw, cooked, or dried. Great for tea and flavoring.

HERBS: MUSTARD FAMILY

SHEPHERD'S PURSE
Capsella bursa-pastoris

Family: Brassicaceae
Lookalikes: Pennycress
WARNING: Can induce uterine contractions, so do not ingest during pregnancy. Avoid if you are taking medication for high blood pressure or have thyroid or heart problems. Possible sedative.

Description
This annual (sometimes biennial) Eurasian immigrant is similar to other mustard family members. It has a cluster of basal mustard or dandelion-like leaves that are deeply lobed. Smaller, unlobed, pointed leaves along the stalk.

Flowers are small and white, with four petals, forming a very loose raceme along the upper portion of the stalk. They appear to be dancing up the stem toward the sky. Seeds are encapsulated in light green seedpods similar to those of pennycress but triangular or heart shaped rather than rounded. Mature plants are sometimes quite small but can reach 12"–18" high. Flowers and seedpods often appear on one plant at the same time.

Range and Habitat
Disturbed areas and fields throughout the plains and foothills of the Rocky Mountains. Widespread throughout the continent.

Comments
This wild mustard family edible is well loved in China and Korea. All parts of the plant are edible. Use greens cooked or in salads. There is great variation on the taste of the seeds. Sometimes strongly mustard flavored, and other times no flavor at all. When flavorful, seeds and seedpods make a great mustardy flavoring, and roots can be used like ginger.

RECIPE

Wild Greens Wontons

The mustard flavor is a great complement to soy dipping sauce, green onions, and shrimp. To make wonton filling, combine 2 cups diced shrimp or tofu, ½ cup diced green onions, ½ cup diced baby bok choy, ½ cup diced mushrooms, 1 egg (beaten), ½ teaspoon fresh-grated ginger, 1 tablespoon soy sauce, ¾ tablespoon sesame oil, and ½ teaspoon organic cornstarch with ¾ cup diced shepherd's purse leaves and/or green seedpods (use less if using the spicy seedpods rather than greens). Mix together well.

Have a bowl of flour and a cup of cool water ready. Use premade wonton wrappers (or make your own). Place a small spoonful of mixture into center of each wonton wrapper. Wet the edges lightly with water. Fold over so that edges meet; squeeze and tuck the sides gently so they stick together. Dip and roll gently in flour, and place on cookie sheets. Can be cooked immediately or frozen (place cookie sheet into freezer and once wontons are frozen, store in sealed containers).

To cook, bring a large pot of water to a rolling boil; add wontons. Stir very gently so the wontons do not stick together. When wontons float to the top, they are ready to serve.

Variation: Fry wontons instead of boiling.

PENNYCRESS
Thlaspi arvense

Family: Brassicaceae
Other names: Frenchweed, stinkweed, fanweed, field pennycress
Lookalikes: Shepherd's purse

Description
This introduced annual member of the mustard family grows 6"–2½' in height. It is hairless with lanceolate, alternate leaves with slightly wavy margins that can have blunted teeth.

Lamb's-Quarter Greens and Pennycress Wrap

These tiny little wraps are packed full of flavor.

Harvest several fresh (not dried out) pennycress seedpods. Also harvest several amaranth leaves, lamb's-quarter leaves, and the thin grass-like leaves of salsify. Place 1 amaranth leaf and 1 lamb's-quarter leaf on top of each other. Place a pennycress seedpod on top. Roll to form a tube or wrap. Tie together with the salsify leaf. Fill a small serving plate with the spicy bundles.

Variation: Add a bit of soft mild cheese to the wraps.

Small, four-petaled flowers are white and form open or wispy, rounded clusters toward the top of the stalk.

Obvious rounded seedpods are light green and flat and often have one small, narrow indentation on the outer edge. Seedpods are thin discs with a large lump in the middle where the seeds reside inside.

Range and Habitat
From Alaska to Florida along roadsides, disturbed areas, open fields, and in gardens. Plains to montane zone.

Comments
Seeds and leaves are edible raw or cooked. This is a common garden weed and a great weed to cultivate.

The leaves are similar in flavor to cultivated mustard greens and are tender, spicy, and delicious. The seeds are a mustard substitute and very similar to,

Pennycress Coconut Soup with Bok Choy and Tofu

In a large saucepan or soup pot, combine one 13.5 fluid ounce can coconut milk, 3 cups water, and 2 vegan bouillon cubes. Add a dash of fish oil and a dash of soy sauce. Add 1 scant teaspoon palm sugar or brown sugar. Also add ½ chopped Thai pepper and 2 tablespoons pennycress seedpods (fresh, not dried). Turn heat to medium.

Add two medium-size purple potatoes and 1 medium-size carrot, both sliced into ¾" cubes. Bring mixture to a simmer; simmer covered for 15 minutes, or until potatoes are tender, stirring periodically.

Meanwhile chop 2 cups bok choy greens and stalks; set aside. Also cut 1½ cups firm tofu into ¾" cubes. Once potatoes are soft, add bok choy and tofu to pot. Simmer covered, stirring a few times, for 8 minutes. Serve hot.

although often far more flavorful and spicy than, grocery store varieties. Eat the entire seedpod before it dries out, or crack open and harvest the seeds after the pod dries. Seeds can be used to flavor any dish or used to make mustard or an edible oil.

FRINGED SAGE
Artemesia frigida

Family: Asteraceae
Other names: Fringed sagewort, pasture sagewort, prairie sagewort, *romerillo del llano*
WARNING: Do not use during pregnancy.

RECIPE

Flower Stalk Tea

Prepare a hot infused tea using flowers from one or two stalks, fresh or dried. Good at onset of a cold or flu. Can be medicinal and is very strong, so do not drink too much without consulting an herbalist. Because it is so strongly flavored, most people will adequately self-monitor and only want to drink small amounts.

Description

Similar to white sage (*A. ludoviciana*) but with much more feathery leaves. Deeply divided leaves form a mat close to the ground 4"–8" high. Leaves are downy silver-green or grayish. The flower stalks grow 12"–18" from the mat of leaves and produce button-like yellow or silvery-yellow flowers. Not likely to flower in drought years.

Range and Habitat

Overgrazed pastures, from the Yukon throughout the Great Basin.

Comments

More mildly flavored than big sagebrush or silver sage. Use leaves and flowering stalks as tea or for a smudge. Less medicinal than other varieties.

WHITE SAGE
Artemesia ludoviciana

Family: Asteraceae

Other names: Wormwood, western mugwort, Louisiana wormwood, cudweed sagewort, gray sagewort, mugwort wormwood, prairie sage, white sagebrush, mariola, alcanfor, estafiate

Related species: Field sagewort/Northern wormwood (*A. campestris*), fringed sage (*A. frigida*), Mexican wormwood (*A. mexicana*)

WARNING: Some people may be allergic. **Do not use during pregnancy.**

FORAGER NOTE: Not to be confused with the Salvia genus of sages. Salvia sages have square stems and are related to mint and culinary sage.

Description

This deliciously pungent erect native perennial generally reaches 2'–3' when mature but is also often seen in young patches just a few inches tall. Can grow to 6'–7', but the weak stems will often flop over if unsupported. Whitish or silvery gray woolly down covers the leaves, giving them their characteristic light-frosted look.

Leaves are linear, up to 4³⁄₁₀" long. Toward the top of the stalk, many tiny nodding flower heads appear in late summer. They have yellow central discs and together form a sparse, narrow inflorescence. They turn brown or reddish brown as they dry out in fall.

Fruits are small, dry achenes. Plants usually grow in clumps spreading from underground rhizomes.

Range and Habitat

Widespread from the Northwest Territories to Texas, across the West to California and much of the eastern United States. Dry fields, roadsides, gardens, forests, and forest edges.

Comments

Leaves, flowers, and seeds can be used as flavoring or for tea. Widely loved as a smudge. Harvest before or during flowering period. Tea can be used as a bitters for a digestive aid and to help with menstrual cramps, inhaled for lung health, and used for other medicinal purposes. It is antifungal and antimalarial. Can also be used as a deodorant and insect repellent.

BIG SAGEBRUSH
Artemisia tridentata

Family: Asteraceae

Other names: Great basin sagebrush, *chamiso hediondo*

WARNING: Some people have negative reactions when this plant is rubbed on skin or taken internally. **Should NOT BE TAKEN in any form (internally or externally) by pregnant women,** as it can help stimulate menstrual flows.

Description

Six subspecies are recognized, including basin big sagebrush (the largest), Wyoming big sagebrush, and mountain big sagebrush. Depending on the subspecies, mature plants are often in the range of 3'–4' high, but in some cases 8'–13' tall. Leaf tips are generally lobed (wavy toothed) but sometimes pointed.

In general, big sagebrush has a woody main stem with vegetative branches reaching upwards, creating an even or uneven top, depending on the subspecies.

Leaves are silvery sage colored and deliciously pungent. They are small, less than 1" long, flat, and wedge shaped, often with three teeth at the flat tips, tapering to the base where they attach to the stem.

Small, discreet yellow flower heads about ⅛" long form together into narrow clusters that stick out from the crown. The clusters are stunted in drought years but otherwise somewhat tall. Achenes are smooth (glabrous) or hairy (less likely).

Range and Habitat
Dominant shrub of the Great Basin region. British Columbia across the West to New Mexico and North Dakota to Nebraska. Valley bottoms, low foothills, and large expanses of dry open plains and hillsides up to the montane zone, especially where rainfall is 12"–18" per year.

Comments
In the windy and sparse high deserts, you would feel alone if not for the big sagebrush welcoming you on every gust of wind. This is the aromatherapy of our region, the historical scent of the West. But don't confuse it with (or substitute it for) culinary sage. Wild sage has a much stronger flavor, although it can certainly be used very sparsely in cooking. The culinary sages, the Salvias , have square stems and are related to mint. The Artemesias are what we think of when we think of desert sages and smudges.

Leaves and seeds can be eaten raw or cooked or made into tea. Seeds can be dried and crushed and used as a flavoring.

The plant has lots of medicinal uses: as a chest compress to break up mucus, a tea to induce sweating and help with viral infections, and an inhalant when sick. Steep in oil and apply to stiff joints (good for arthritis), or make a footbath and soak. Also good to simmer in hot water and inhale aromatics when you have a cold. High in volatile oils, so steep tea with lid on. Sagebrush tea is very strong; only very small amounts should be consumed. **CAUTION:** Gagging can result if overconsumed.

Sagebrush is also a disinfectant and can be used as a cleaning agent in the home, used as a tea poured over wounds to clean them, or burned to purify the air. It is also somewhat sedative. Rub on skin as insect repellent and perfume, or chew a few leaves to help with illness or to freshen breath.

WILD CARAWAY
Carum spp.

Family: Apiaceae

Other names: Meridian fennel, Persian cumin, *C. carvi* (white flower), *C. trachypleura* (yellow flower)

Lookalikes: Yarrow, Poison hemlock (*Conium maculatum*), water hemlock (*Cicuta maculata*); any of the white-umbelled species, including osha (*Ligusticum porteri*), osha del campo (Angelica; *Angelica grayi*), Queen Anne's lace (*Daucus carota*), wild parsleys (*Lomatium* spp.), water parsnip (*Sium suave*)

WARNING: Some sources warn that excessive use of caraway can lead to kidney and liver problems. Use in moderation as you would any seasoning.

Do not confuse with the deadly lookalikes poison hemlock and water hemlock.

Description

Wild caraway is a biennial (sometimes three-year, sometimes perennial) herb with a parsley-like basal rosette in its first year. In the second year, one or more straw-colored or purplish stalks, 1'–3' tall, arise from each taproot. Taproots are small, up to about ½" thick.

The stalk is lined with deeply divided, feathery, somewhat carrot-like alternate leaves. *C. carvi* has white or pinkish flowers that form flat-topped clusters or umbels 1½"–4½" wide at the top of each stalk. *C. trachypleura* has similar but yellow flowers.

Wild caraway fruits (achenes) look like store-bought caraway seeds. They are notable by their distinct, pale-colored linear ribs or ridges. They are brown, narrow, and crescent shaped.

The photo is of the less-common species of wild caraway, *C. trachypleur*, which has more-rounded, less–crescent shaped seeds than *C. carvi*.

Range and Habitat

Dry to moist, disturbed areas, pastures, roadsides, and ditches. Sun or dappled shade. Plains and mountainous regions up to at least 9,000' in elevation. *C. trachypleur* is limited to a narrow band along the eastern slope of the Rockies. *C. carvi* is much more widespread.

RECIPE

Grilled Beets and Turnips with Wild Caraway Seed

Early fall, when the beets are huge and the caraway seeds are drying on their stalks, is the right time for some long-shadowed barbecues on the back deck.

Preheat grill. Harvest garden-fresh beets and turnips, and scrub off the dirt. Slice thickly into rounds, and place in bowl. Add some olive oil and tamari. With your hands, massage oil mixture into vegetables.

Grill over medium heat, turning every few minutes. Begin cooking beets before turnips, as they take longer to cook.

Place fresh-picked parsley in bowl with remaining oil-tamari mixture, and toss like a salad.

When root vegetables are just browned, remove from grill and place directly onto the bed of parsley. Garnish with plenty of wild caraway seeds.

Comments

Designated as a noxious weed in Colorado, which means it is "required to be either eradicated, contained, or suppressed." Crazy. The seeds are used around the world as a flavoring in sauerkraut, pudding, curry, and liquors and as an after-meal digestive aid. Leaves are less flavorful than seeds. Use leaves as a salad green or cooked. The root is also edible like any root vegetable and has a stronger flavor than parsnip.

QUEEN ANNE'S LACE
Daucus carota

Family: Apiaceae
Other names: Wild carrot, bird's nest (because the old flower umbel curls into a bird's-nest shape), bishop's lace
Lookalikes: Poison hemlock (*Conium maculatum*), water hemlock (*Cicuta maculata*), osha (*Ligusticum porteri*), osha del campo (Angelica; *Angelica grayi*), wild parsleys (*Lomatium* spp.), water parsnip (*Sium suave*)
WARNING: Very easy to confuse with deadly lookalikes poison hemlock and water hemlock. Foragers in our region recently have died because of this confusion.

I cannot absolutely confirm that no other lookalike has this purple marking, but none that I know of do.

FORAGER NOTE: One of the easiest of the white-umbelled lookalikes to identify because of the tiny red or dark purple flower in the center of the umbel—the drop of blood spilled in the center of the umbel as Queen Anne was sewing her lace. The "blood" droplet is actually a single, tiny, dark colored flower right in the middle of the white umbel.

Description

This biennial creates a first-year basal rosette that looks similar to the leaves of a cultivated carrot. The parsley- or fern-like leaves are low growing, although with competition they stand more upright. In the second year the stalk reaches 2'–6' tall. The stalk is sometimes branched, especially toward the top. The stem can be distinguished from that of poison hemlock because it is solid (not hollow) and does not have a white coating (bloom). Hairy stem is light green with purple stripes.

When flowering, the plant is typically shorter than poison hemlock, which more commonly grows 6'–9' tall. Leaves and stem of wild carrot are noticeably hairy, whereas poison hemlock is hairless.

Umbels form mostly at or toward the top of the plant (rather than from the middle upwards, like poison hemlock), although stands often have shorter and taller plants, so there is an illusion of flowers growing from the middle. Flower clusters consist of about thirty umbellets that form the umbel, which is about 5" across. The center umbellet often contains a single purple flower.

Far thinner and more delicate looking that the similar angelica.

Range and Habitat

Grows very sparsely throughout the Rocky Mountain region. Keep this in mind when you think you have found wild carrot. It is more likely to be one of the

Hearty Wild Game Stew

In a slow cooker combine 3 cups bite-size squares of wild game of choice (or beef), 2 to 4 cups thickly sliced wild carrot, thickly sliced celery (3 stalks) and ¼ cup dried barley. Add plenty of fresh-ground black pepper and sea salt, ¼ teaspoon turmeric, and several fresh, peeled garlic cloves. I also like to add a jalapeño or other spicy pepper. Cook on high all day, about 8 to 10 hours.

Variation: Add 1 tablespoon honey or molasses.

deadly poisonous lookalikes. Much more common in the Midwest and eastern United States. Considered a noxious weed in the Midwest, even though the plant is edible and provides an important food source for pollinators. Be sure to find out whether stands are sprayed with herbicide by your local authorities before consuming. Grows in open fields, dry areas, ditches, and disturbed sites. Prefers the lower elevations of the plains regions throughout the Rockies.

Comments

The root, young shoots, and seeds are edible. The root is white or cream colored and smells like a carrot. Use it as you would a domestic carrot, although I recommend trying it raw before cooking, just to get a real sense of the similarities and differences.

Daucus carota is the ancestor of the domesticated carrot, and relatives are known to have been cultivated in Iran in the tenth century and in Northern Africa and Syria by the eleventh century. Many European paintings from the 1600s include depictions of carrots. This is a widespread edible food and has been for thousands of years.

Bring a shovel to dig the roots. Be sure to harvest the correct root.

RECIPE

Carrot and Parsley Salad

Finely chop equal amounts young wild carrot and parsley shoots. Toss well with olive oil, sweet rice vinegar, and a dash of soy sauce.

COW PARSNIP
Heracleum maximum

Family: Apiaceae

Other names: Indian celery, pushki, *H. lanatum, H. sphondylium*

Lookalikes: Poison hemlock (*Conium maculatum*), water hemlock (*Cicuta maculata*), osha (*Ligusticum porteri*), osha del campo (Angelica; *Angelica grayi*), Queen Anne's lace (*Daucus carota*), wild parsleys (*Lomatium* spp.), water parsnip (*Sium suave*), devil's club (leaves), baneberry (leaves)

WARNING: Do not confuse with water hemlock or poison hemlock, which are DEADLY poisonous.

Be careful when harvesting, as the sap of cow parsnip on the skin can cause serious reactions and blistering when exposed to sunlight. This is called phytophotodermatitis and looks like dark splotches on the skin. Covering the skin with long sleeves and gloves before harvesting is recommended.

Description

This tall, robust native perennial grows from 3½'–10' tall. Large, flat-topped (or somewhat rounded) white

FORAGER NOTE: Its huge leaves distinguish cow parsnip from other carrot family members.

umbels of flowers are pungent and grow 8"–12" wide. The large, rounded maple leaf–shaped (palmate but not deeply lobed) leaves are 8"–20" wide. Egg-shaped fruit is less than 1" long.

This is one of the easier to identify of the white-umbelled lookalikes, as the leaves are uniquely palmate (not fern-like or parsley-like) and huge compared with other carrot family relatives.

Range and Habitat

Moist or wet soil from Alaska to New Mexico in plains, foothills, forests, subalpine and montane regions, and especially in riparian areas. Up to about 10,000' in elevation.

RECIPE

Ants on a Log

A wild twist on an old favorite and a great trail snack.

Peel raw stalks, and spread peanut butter along the stem. Press plump raisins onto the peanut butter.

Sautéed Stalks and Leaf Stems

Harvest 3 cups young stalks and leaf stems. Peel and slice into 3" to 5" sections; set aside.

Heat a large skillet to medium high heat. Add 1½ tablespoons olive oil. Add 3 cloves fresh garlic, chopped, and gently sauté for 3 minutes. Add cow parsnip stalks and petioles; sauté until soft, about 8 minutes, stirring frequently. Remove from heat. Add a dash of salt and crushed, dried roasted hot peppers.

Comments

Young, hollow stems can be peeled and eaten raw, roasted (unpeeled), boiled, steamed, or dipped in sugar. They taste like celery and also somewhat like rhubarb but are not good when older. The roots are also edible and taste similar to rutabagas or parsnip. Roots can be made into tea or a poultice. Young leaves are edible. Roots can be boiled to extract the sugar. Insides of stems can be eaten raw or cooked.

Good forage for elk, mule deer, and small mammals.

OSHA
Ligusticum porteri

Family: Apiaceae

Other names: Bear root, Porter's lovage, chuchupate, osha of the mountains, coughroot, Colorado coughroot

Lookalikes: Poison hemlock (*Conium maculatum*), water hemlock (*Cicuta maculata*), osha del campo (Angelica; *Angelica grayi*), Queen Anne's lace (*Daucus carota*), wild parsleys (*Lomatium* spp.), water parsnip (*Sium suave*), Gairdner's yampah (*Perideridia gairdneri*)

Also similar to Canby's licorice-root, or Canby's lovage (*Ligusticum canbyi*), also sometimes called osha, which is only found in the northwestern United States and British Columbia.

WARNING: Do not confuse with deadly lookalikes poison hemlock and water hemlock.

The root of osha is strong and medicinal. Use with care. The root might be too strong for use during pregnancy.

Description

This tall, pungent native perennial has erect hollow stems with white flat-topped flower heads.

Large upright or upward-arching fern- or parsley-like leaves grow along the stalk. They are larger and denser, up to 2'–3' high, becoming much smaller and sparser on the upper half of the stalk. The largest leaves can reach up to about 2' long. Leaves are alternate, with a strong carroty or parsley scent. Young leaves emerge in a tight ruffly cluster and eventually unfurl. Leaves are green but turn yellow, orange, or reddish in fall. Leaf veins terminate at the tips or points of the teeth (like poison hemlock), not in the margins or dips between the points (like water hemlock).

A hollow erect stem emerges from the cluster of basal leaves and grows 2'–6' tall. The stem is green and can have purple splotches or markings. The root is brown and has obvious remnants of past years' growth, which forms a fibrous, thick, peeling, hair-like skin around the fresh root.

Flowers in late summer. Flower heads emerge as tight whitish umbels and unfurl to become wider, white flat-topped compound umbels.

One way to distinguish this plant from its poisonous relatives is by its strong carrot smell. However, be aware that it can grow interspersed with poison hemlock or the poisonous water hemlock, and its smell can overwhelm the area, making it difficult to tell which plants do not share the scent. Be sure to use ALL other factors in making an identification.

Range and Habitat

Grows from about 5,000'–10,000' in elevation. It is found in moist high-altitude areas, especially with some dappled shade, mostly in the Four Corners region. Often grows in dense patches under aspen groves. More sparsely found in Montana, Idaho, Wyoming, and Nevada.

Many sources claim that osha and poison hemlock grow at different altitudes; however, this is not the case and can't be relied on for identification.

Comments

Osha is a plant only for advanced foragers. It is listed here only so that readers can be aware of this wonderful and well-loved herb. It so closely resembles several deadly poisonous plants that you should absolutely not plan on consuming it unless you have been trained by someone with significant expertise. This is not something like dandelion or raspberry, or even the similar-looking cow parsnip, that you can be confident in identifying with just the advice of books and some careful investigation.

I do, however, recommend searching for it and using that search to hone your plant identification skills. Thinking about the significant consequences of an incorrect ID will get your heart pumping and will keep your senses alert as you go through each piece of the identification puzzle.

Boiled Honey and Osha Root

This recipe was shared with me by John Duncan, founder of the Oso Negro School and adjunct professor of Wild Food and Wild Medicine at the University of New Mexico, Taos.

Heat about 2 cups good honey and ½ cup chopped and dried Osha root in a double boiler to a very low simmer. Simmer together about 30 to 60 minutes. Store in an airtight jar through winter, and take a small spoon of the honey when you feel a sore throat coming on. You can use the honey in tea or in a mug of hot water.

The small chucks of root can be eaten. They can also be used like a cough drop or steeped to make tea. Spoon a piece of root out of the honey mixture and suck or chew it. Much better for you than the sugary and artificially colored cough drops from the store.

Variation: For a raw honey variation, chop dried osha root into small pieces and mix into a jar of raw, liquid honey. Store in sealed jar; use the same way as described above.

This plant is very difficult, but not impossible, to cultivate.

Leaves, roots, and seeds are edible. Leaves can be eaten raw, cooked, or dried. They can be considered medicinal but are mildly so and can be eaten like any green. The seeds are a spicy celery flavor and are good to use as a seasoning cooked or raw. The roots are very strong and are medicinal, not food. Root is used dried as a tea, decoction, or tincture for coughs, congestion, and other medicinal purposes.

A traditional native food use is to pick osha leaves prior to flowering. They are then dried and used in soups and stews.

Osha Root Tea

Bring water to a boil. Place osha root pieces into tea strainer and pour boiling water over it. Steep for 7–10 minutes. Drink slowly at the first onset of a cold or sore throat. Excellent with a spoonful of honey and dried peppermint leaves.

NARROWLEAF YUCCA
Yucca glauca

Family: Agavaceae
Other names: Soapwort, soapweed, Spanish bayonet, Great Plains yucca, needle palm
Lookalikes: Century plant (*Agave americana*), sotol (*Dasylirion wheeleri*), agave (*Agave*), banana yucca (*Y. baccata*)
Related species: Narrowleaf yucca (*Y. angustissima, Y. harrimaniae*)
WARNING: Pregnant women should not drink tea made from the roots, as it can induce labor. High saponin levels in the roots can make them toxic in large amounts.

FORAGER NOTE: Yucca glauca, or narrowleaf yucca, shares a similar name with an entirely different food plant. It is not the same as the starchy, potato-like root eaten widely across the Caribbean, South America, and parts of Africa, called Yuca (*Manihot esculenta*). Yuca is also called cassava, manioc, and tapioca.

Description

This common native perennial is a showy evergreen subshrub. It has very stiff, erect basal leaves that angle slightly outwards to form a dense, rounded cluster from which an erect stem emerges and produces a white, cream, or green-tinged cluster of bell-shaped flowers. Flowers are large, bulbous, and form a tight panicle cluster toward the top of the stalk. The stalk grows 1½'–5' tall. Blooms late spring to summer.

Leaves are simple, stiff, linear, and needle or sword like. The very fibrous leaves grow 1'–5' long and form in clusters 2'–4' wide. Leaves shed along their margins and have fibrous strings curling along the edges. Fruits are hardened, ovular, cream or light greenish capsules about 2½" long.

Range and Habitat

Rocky areas with full sun exposure throughout dry plains and foothills from Alberta to Texas. Hardy to USDA Zone 4. Thrives in sandy and poor soil conditions. Can be found up to about 8,500' elevation and are often seen along roadsides and disturbed areas.

RECIPE

Yucca Flower Veggie Sauté

Peel 1 cup petals off the flower's central core. Bring a pot of water to a boil, and boil flower petals for 15 to 20 minutes. Strain.

In a saucepan heat 1 teaspoon canola oil; add the following chopped vegetables: 1 tomato, 1 onion, 2 cloves garlic, and 1 green pepper. Add the boiled flower petals and 1 teaspoon honey or sugar. Stir to combine. Simmer for 15 minutes, slightly covered. Serve with warm tortillas or corn chips.

Yucca Shampoo

Add ½ cup yucca root (fresh or dried) to 1½ cups water. Boil until mixture becomes sudsy. Remove from heat, and use as you would any shampoo.
   Variation: Can also be made using cold water.

Comments

The flowers, flower buds, and young stalks are edible. Flowers can be eaten raw, dried, boiled, or fried. Use only the petals, and discard the bitter green inside part. The flower stem can be used like asparagus, much like the stem of salsify. I have read reports that the leaves can be eaten, but they are very fibrous so require long baking or boiling. Seed pods may be edible, but this is not confirmed.

Narrowleaf yucca is the state flower of New Mexico and is commonly referred to as soapweed because the roots can be pounded and mixed with water to make soap. The root can be made into a tea and used medicinally for inflammation and arthritis.

Narrowleaf yucca has a symbiotic pollination relationship with the night-flying yucca moth.

Its relative, the banana yucca (*Yucca baccata*) has large, soft, sweet fruits that are excellent to eat. Banana yucca is found from California to New Mexico and Texas and into Mexico.

CREEPING AMARANTH
Amaranthus blitoides

Family: Amaranthaceae
Other names: Prostrate pigweed, mat amaranth, matweed
Lookalikes: Somewhat like purslane and chickweed
WARNING: Can accumulate nitrogen when grown in high-nitrogen soils. Avoid eating from locations where nitrogen fertilizer is used, as it can cause problems such as blue-baby syndrome.

Description
This prostrate, creeping annual reaches a height of only about 8" tall and can spread about 2' wide. Thick, succulent red or whitish stems crisscross along the ground. Spoon-shaped leaves are cupped and ringed in white around the edges (although some varieties of this species have leaves that are not cupped and do not have the white rim). Leaves form in clusters off stem shoots and are attached by small petioles. Flowers in late summer or early fall and then sets seeds in fall.

Range and Habitat
Found widely across the United States, especially on disturbed ground. Grows up to 8,500' in elevation, probably higher.

Comments

Leaves and stems can be eaten raw or cooked like spinach. Seeds can be eaten whole or crushed and exude a gelatinous substance when mixed into soups. The seeds of the creeping amaranth hide behind the leaves and are not terribly worth collecting except for investigative purposes.

RECIPE

Creeping Amaranth Macaroni and Cheese

Harvest 1 cup leaves of creeping amaranth by stripping leaves from the stalks. Wash well in cool water to remove dirt.

In a medium-size saucepan combine 1 cup organic milk with 2 tablespoons butter, ½ teaspoon salt, and ½ teaspoon fresh-ground black pepper. Heat until mixture just begins to bubble; reduce heat to prevent boiling. Add the amaranth leaves, and stir for about 2 minutes. Then add 1 cup cheddar cheese and ¼ cup Gorgonzola cheese to saucepan. Allow cheese to melt, but do not boil. Stir periodically to prevent sticking.

Meanwhile, boil water and cook small shell-shaped pasta according to package instructions. Drain pasta, and add hot cheese sauce. Mix gently but thoroughly. Top with grated chopped, garden-fresh parsley.

RECIPE

Kasha with Creeping Amaranth

Kasha reminds me of my Grandma Buddy's house. Here's a simple wild twist on an old favorite. Kasha is buckwheat and is gluten free. Kasha has a strong, earthy flavor and is good mixed with other more mildly flavored foods. Traditionally, it is made in a dish with bow-tie pasta.

Rinse 1 cup kasha in water. Bring 2 cups water to a boil. Add the kasha, and reduce heat to a simmer. Simmer covered for 15 minutes. Remove from heat and let stand with lid on for 10 minutes.

In a separate large bowl, add 1 cup creeping amaranth leaves. Cut the kernels off of 2 to 3 cobs of organic sweet corn. Add to bowl. Chop 1 apple into small, bite-size squares. Add to bowl. Add 2 tablespoons olive oil and the juice of 1 large lemon. Toss veggie-apple mixture so that all ingredients are coated evenly with the oil and lemon juice. Add the warm kasha; toss well. Salt and pepper to taste. Add dried roasted hot peppers if desired. Enjoy cold or at room temperature.

Variation: Substitute raw or grilled plums for the apple.

COMMON AMARANTH
Amaranthus retroflexus

Family: Amaranthaceae

Other names: Pigweed, redroot pigweed, wild beet, green amaranth

WARNING: Contains oxalates. See oxalates discussion in introduction. Can accumulate nitrates, which can be extremely toxic. Avoid eating amaranth that has been grown in areas that have received high doses of nitrogen fertilizer.

Description

This common annual grows from about 8"–8' tall. Affected by moisture, in particularly dry or compacted soils it will be on the shorter side.

Green flowers lack petals and form cone-shaped clusters along the stalk, especially at the top. Flower clusters can reach 11" long but will be smaller on smaller plants. They contain sharp, spine-like bracts when dry.

Fruits are tiny and contain one seed each. Tiny seeds are shiny and black (sometimes dark brown). Leaves hang from petioles and are alternate, ovate (oval) with a somewhat pointed tip or diamond shaped, and ½"–5" long.

Range and Habitat

From Alaska southward throughout the United States. Found on plains up to the montane zone, especially in gardens and other disturbed sites. There are numerous species of amaranth in United States.

Comments

Leaves and seeds are edible. Harvest seeds by beating them out of their pods and winnowing off the chaff. Rinse and allow to dry, and then toast lightly or eat raw. Leaves can be eaten raw, dried, or cooked. Leaves can also be dried and ground into a green powder for a nutritious addition to smoothies.

RECIPE

Green Juice

I learned this method for making wild green juice from Katrina Blair, founder of Turtle Lake Refuge, a wild foods mecca in Durango, Colorado.

Harvest leaves from a variety of wild greens like dandelions, thistle, amaranth, wheatgrass, yarrow, or whatever you find growing. (**NOTE:** Harvesting just a couple of leaves per plant does not harm the plant.) Place all leaves in a blender filled with good water. Blend on high until greens are pulverized, about 2 minutes. Strain and retain the green juice. Store in a glass jar with a lid in the refrigerator for a day or two. Drink one or more times per day, especially before meals. Best to sip slowly about 30 minutes before eating.

RECIPE

Amaranth Leaf Quesadilla

Start with a large, very soft whole-wheat tortilla. Lay tortilla out on a cutting board, and cover half with a layer of cleaned, chopped amaranth leaves. Cover with cheese or cheese substitute. Add sliced tomatoes and fresh chopped garlic. Sprinkle with fresh-ground pepper.

Heat 1 tablespoon olive oil in large skillet. Fold empty side of tortilla over side with fillings. Place in hot skillet and fry over medium-high heat until just brown. Flip and repeat until the other side is lightly browned. Remove from heat and cut into pizza-like slices. Sprinkle truffle oil lightly on top; sprinkle with salt if desired.

Variation: Use organic corn tortillas instead. Corn tortillas are usually small. If using corn tortillas, do not fold in half. Instead, lay one tortilla out flat. Place amaranth leaves, cheese, and other fillings inside. Cover with another tortilla. Fry in pan as described.

SHOWY MILKWEED
Asclepias speciosa

Family: Asclepiadaceae
Other names: Showy milkweed
Lookalikes: Dogbane, false hellebore (*Veratrum* spp.; **poisonous**)
Related species: Common milkweed (*A. syriaca*), found in the Midwest and East, with some range overlap
WARNING: Do not consume raw sap. White milky sap in all parts of the plant is toxic raw but perfectly safe when cooked. **Many sources warn not to consume brown seeds.** Seeds and seedpods are edible (cooked) when young, but older brown seeds are reported to be toxic. Avoid getting sap in your eyes.

Several species of false hellebore (*Veratrum* spp.) have the potential to be confused with showy milkweed. Both have thick, erect stalks; grow 2'–4' tall; and have very large, thick leaves. Hellebore leaves are deeply ridged and look somewhat like big fat pieces of lettuce that would make a great burrito wrap. Don't be fooled. **This plant is poisonous and should not be consumed.**

Description

This native perennial stands on a thick, erect, hairy stalk 2'–5' tall. Large ovate leaves on short petioles are opposite and have a pronounced light-pinkish or cream-colored midvein. Leaves grow up to 8" long. Plant reaches 2'–3' tall.

Terminal clusters of showy, star-shaped pink flowers bloom in midsummer. Flower hoods (arms of the star) are long and pointed. Compare with common milkweed, which has short hoods. A large, distinct seedpod or follicle points upwards. It is bumpy, like it is covered in warts, and contains many flat, tightly packed seeds attached to shiny, white, silky plumes.

RECIPE

Boiled Young Seedpods

Pay attention to a local stand of milkweed. When the seedpods just begin to appear, that is the right time to harvest them. Do not harvest when the seeds are brown or when the silk inside becomes dry and inedible.

Place seedpods in a large pot of boiling water; boil for 20 minutes. Remove from pot and toss with fresh herbs, olive oil or butter, and a pinch of sea salt.

Stir-fry with Milkweed Flowers

Harvest young flowers, which are somewhat like broccolini heads.

Heat vegetable oil in a wok over high heat. Add garlic, and sizzle. Add diced milkweed flower heads. (I like to leave them whole so that you get the full visual of what the plant looks like.) Sauté until tender.

Serve over fresh brown rice with soy sauce and diced green onions.

Range and Habitat

Native to the western half of the United States. Found from British Columbia to Texas, from sea level to 9,000' in elevation. Grows in areas with some moisture, such as roadside ditches, moist fields, or other poorly drained areas.

Comments

Young shoots, stems, flower buds, flowers, and young leaves can be eaten, usually boiled. Very young seedpods (seeds must be white.) and roots can also be eaten, again, usually boiled. Oil can also be consumed. Milkweed vegetables have a taste somewhat like peas, tomatillos, or very mild roasted green chilies.

Be sure to cook well. Milky sap (latex) should not be eaten raw, although some people eat very small amounts raw without obvious signs of problems. Safe when cooked thoroughly.

Several sources warn that the brown seeds are toxic and should not be eaten. I have not been able to confirm this.

Many people like to harvest wearing gloves to keep the milky sap off of their skin and clothes. Old dried stalks can be made into cord, rope, netting, and coarse fabric.

Attracts butterflies, bees, and a variety of other insects. Milkweed is especially important to the Monarch butterfly, as it's one of the very few plants Monarchs will lay their eggs on. Eggs are laid on the underside of dense patches of leaves, and the larvae will eventually build their chrysalis on the milkweed. Milkweed sap contains chemicals that are thought to make Monarchs unappealing to would-be predators.

The silky down of the seedpods is several times more buoyant than cork and can be used to stuff life jackets, pillows, and cushions. Root is used medicinally.

PRICKLY PEAR CACTI
Opuntia spp.

Family: Cactaceae

Related species: Plains prickly pear cactus (*O. polyacantha*), brittle prickly pear cactus (*O. fragilis*)

Other names: Nopal, nopales, paddle cactus, tuna cactus, Indian fig

WARNING: Large thorns are obvious; tiny thorns are not so obvious. Gloves are recommended.

Description

This native evergreen perennial consists of about 200 species of prickly pear cacti. Different species readily hybridize.

Clusters of flat, rounded, fleshy stems (cladodes) that are like paddles or beaver tails make up the body of the prickly pear. Leaves are tiny and short-lived. Many species are low shrubs, found in expanding clumps, although some have woody trunks with the green paddles clustering toward the top. Paddles are mucilaginous inside, like aloe.

Tiny barbed thorn-like hairs (glochids) often go unnoticed, as the larger spines are more obvious. Avoid both. The small hairs can become lodged in the skin for several days.

Large, showy flowers are usually yellow but sometimes pink, reddish, or purple. Below the flowers, in late summer or fall, emerge fleshy fruits whose size and sweetness vary with species. Fruits are pink or red, sometimes green, yellow, or purple, with seeds inside.

Range and Habitat
Deserts and dry grasslands from British Columbia to Texas and Mexico.

Comments
All members of this species are edible. The sweet red fruit, often called tuna or pear, is the most desirable part of the prickly pear. The mucilaginous vegetable portion, called the nopale, or pad, is found inside the green paddle-like stem. It also is edible and delicious, tasting somewhat like tart green beans.

Flower petals and seeds are also edible. When harvesting flower petals, take only a few. Leave the reproductive parts intact to allow the fruit to form.

RECIPE

Grilled Nopale Salsa

Remove prickly skin as described above. Lightly coat inner flesh with oil. Grill gently until just browned. Remove from heat and dice. Combine with equal parts diced, raw tomatoes. Add chopped onion, chopped garlic, and plenty of fresh-squeezed lime juice. Salt and pepper to taste. Serve with grilled chicken or organic corn chips.

RECIPE

Tuna Fruit Salad

Prepare fruit by stripping the skin as described above. Cut into quarters or, if very large fruits, bite-size pieces. Prepare 2 cups of the cactus fruit. Prepare 1 cup sliced bananas. Squeeze fresh lime juice over the bananas, and toss together gently. Slice enough peaches to make 1 cup. Combine all fruit, and toss gently. Top with pine nuts; serve at room temperature.

Nopales should be harvested when they are firm, not wrinkled. In some species the fruits are big, sweet, and fleshy; in others, less so. Fruits are made into juice, jam, and wine or eaten raw. Pads also can be eaten raw, grilled, or sautéed.

To harvest the fruit or pad, use a sharp knife and make a clean slice about 1" above where it attached to the pad below. Carefully peel the outer layer off the fleshy interior by making one cut down the length and then removing strips of skin with a sharp knife. It is advisable to wear thick protective gloves. To harvest the pads you must remove the small spines, or glochids. The skin can be stripped or left on. Spines can also be scrubbed off with a stiff brush, burned off, or rolled in sand to remove.

Prickly pear is a great survival food because of its high water content and, if needed, can help stave off dehydration. In such a circumstance, be particularly careful about pricking yourself with the spines, because if your body is severely compromised, even a small cut can become infected and turn deadly.

The mucilaginous inside portion of the paddle can also be used as a lotion or salve.

HAREBELL
Campanula rotundifolia

Family: Campanulaceae
Other names: Bluebells of Scotland, bluebell bellflower

Description

This lovely native perennial in the bellflower family produces lavender colored, bell-shaped flowers. Flower heads are five-lobed and dangle downward like a bell from delicate, erect green stalks. Stalks grow to about 1' 4" tall. Often two or more flowers droop in loose clusters from each stalk.

RECIPE

Harebell Leaf Salad

Cut a few leaves from the stalk and add to a salad. The leaves are small, and an all-harebell leaf salad is probably impractical, especially considering its vulnerability.

Leaves are denser toward the bottom of the stalk, becoming sparser toward the top. Leaves are like small, delicate blades of grass attached to the stem to about halfway up and can remain green even after early frosts.

Range and Habitat

Edges of woods or grassy areas, dappled shade or full sun. Hardy to USDA Zone 3 and found from Alaska to Texas and throughout the United States except the Southeast.

Comments

Harebells grow in clusters but usually in small clusters. They are considered endangered or vulnerable in some states. It is important to consider this plant a delicacy and harvest only very small amounts—but a delicacy it surely is.

Leaves, raw or cooked, and flowers are edible. The flowers are like fresh forest candy, and just one will turn your day around. There's just no way not to be happy after sampling just one sweet harebell flower. The root can be chewed for medicinal purposes (heart and lung) or made into a decoction and used as eardrops.

RECIPE

Romantic Vanilla Cake with Harebell Blossom

I am a sucker for a good vanilla cupcake with a hint of almond extract and white frosting. It's a perfect addition to a romantic mid- to late-summer picnic with your special someone. Pick the vanilla cupcake recipe of your choice. Bake and let cool, and frost with homemade vanilla icing. Top with just a few purple harebell flowers, and enjoy.

ROSEROOT
Sedum integrifolium and *S. rhodanthum*

Family: Crassulaceae

Other names: King's crown (*S. integrifolium, Rhodiola integrifolia*), queen's crown (*S. rhodanthum, R. rhodantha*), New Mexico stonecrop, Leedy's roseroot, ledge stonecrop, *Rhodiola neomexicana, Sedum roseum, Sedum rosea*

Description
Native succulent perennial with broad, flat, thick leaves that crowd the stem. Leaves are fleshy and ovate, can be smooth or toothed, and vary in size by subspecies, typically less than 1" long. Erect stems 1"–9" tall grow in clusters. Leaves are

FORAGER NOTE: Formerly in the *Sedum* genus, this group of plants was moved to *Rhodiola* for a while. Based on Jennifer Ackerfield's most recent work, it now seems to be moved back with the sedums. There is significant discrepancy on this however.

Warm Green Salad with Crisp Leeks

Harvest 2 cups of young shoots and leaves. Remove leaves from shoots. Heat oven or toaster oven to 350°F.

Thinly slice 1 cup leeks, and place in a bowl rubbed with a small amount of olive oil to just coat. Toss with sea salt. Place on baking pan; bake until beginning to brown and the ends are crisp. Remove and set aside.

Meanwhile, chop 1 cup baby spinach, ¼ cup dandelion leaves, and ½ cup baby kale.

Heat 1 tablespoon mild-flavored olive oil in skillet over medium-high heat. Toss in the roseroot shoots and leaves, and the dandelion leaves. Toss and then sauté for 5 minutes. Add the kale and sauté until all greens are wilted, just a few more minutes. Add the spinach and toss in. Allow to wilt, about 1 minute.

Remove from heat and serve topped with the crisped leeks.

alternate along the stalk but appear whorled, as the alternate rows are not evenly lined up. Leaves are green, sometimes with a bluish-white powdery coating.

Inflorescences are terminal (at the top of the stalk) clusters of pink, rose, or dark red flowers. They are flattish to rounded. Flowers bloom in mid- to late summer. Red flowers are king's crown; pink flowers are queen's crown.

Range and Habitat
Roseroot prefers cool, high-altitude locations. It is found from Alaska and Newfoundland to the mountains of New Mexico and in some locations in the eastern United States. Grows in moist areas along rocky slopes, open meadows, creekbanks, and high-altitude riparian zones. Found in the arctic and in alpine and subalpine zones from about 9,500'–12,000' in elevation.

Comments
Leaves, shoots, flowers, and roots are edible raw, pickled, or cooked. The juicy leaves can provide water in survival situations and are high in vitamins A and C. Slightly bitter tasting; use like greens or asparagus. Similar to stonecrop but taller and not quite as delicious to eat, but still very good.

Several varieties are considered endangered or threatened because of warming temperatures or habitat destruction. Keep this in mind, and only harvest when you find a large, healthy stand.

Used medicinally for stress relief.

STONECROP
Sedum lanceolatum

Family: Crassulaceae
Other names: Lance-leaved stonecrop, spear-leaf stonecrop, yellow stonecrop
Lookalikes: Wormleaf stonecrop (*S. stenopetalum*) is also edible.
WARNING: Some sources warn of possible stomach upset when large quantities are consumed.

Description
This native perennial is short and succulent, with showy yellow flowers. Hairless, erect, succulent stalks about 2–8" high. Fat, linear, alternate leaves grow closely along the stalk, creating a whorled appearance. Leaves are small, up to about 1" long and also form a basal rosette. Stalks and leaves are either green or pink-red.

Bright yellow buds become bright yellow flowers at the top of each stalk. Flowers have five narrow yellow petals, usually seen in short clusters.

Range and Habitat
Found from the Yukon to New Mexico. Open, rocky hillsides from sea level to the subalpine zone.

Comments

Called lance-leaf stonecrop to distinguish from its relative, roseroot, which is also a succulent but has flattened leaves. Leaves and shoots can be eaten raw, pickled, or cooked. Roots can be roasted or boiled. The plant is mucilagenous, much like mallow or okra, and has a pleasant cucumber-like flavor.

Leaves can be used as a poultice for bites and rashes by mashing them into a ball. Tea can be made from the leaves, stems, and flowers. This tea is said to be used to clean out the womb after childbirth. Some sources also report that stonecrop has some laxative effect.

RECIPE

Salty Fish Salad

Harvest young stalks and leaves of stonecrop. Chop into small bite-size pieces.

Combine in a bowl with smoked oysters (drained if from a can) or smoked trout cut into bite-size pieces. Add finely chopped parsley and a touch of olive oil and vinegar. Toss together gently.

Variations: Add cherry tomatoes cut in half, and toss together with rest of mixture. Add chopped red onion.

MORMON TEA
Ephedra spp.

Family: Ephedraceae
Other names: Joint fir, American ephedra
Lookalikes: Horsetail
Related species: Species include *E. viridis* (most common), *E. torreyana*, and *E. cutleri*.
WARNING: If buying Mormon tea in a store, be careful that you are not purchasing Chinese ephedra (also called ma huang), which is a *much* more potent drug.

RECIPE

Mormon Tea

Harvest plenty of Mormon tea, and dry in cool dark place with adequate airflow. Store dried stems in an airtight jar. The herb will remain more potent if left whole until ready to use, but it also can be ground or chopped into smaller pieces.

Place a spoonful of dried herb into a tea strainer. Add boiling water, and steep until desired strength.

Variation: Add lemon balm, clover, alfalfa, peppermint leaves, rose hips, or honey.

Description

This native evergreen is a small to medium-size green, broom-like shrub growing to 6' tall. Jointed stems are numerous, branching, and crisscrossing. Stems have tiny, scaled leaves that are ⅕" long and barely noticeable. Yellow pollen sacs are prominent in spring. The female plants have green seedpods.

One or several spore-producing cones emerge from the nodes. Leaves and bracts are grouped in two to three, depending on species.

Range and Habitat

From southwestern Wyoming and western Colorado to Arizona and New Mexico. Also in parts of Oregon and California. Desert, dry foothills, mountain grasslands, piñon-juniper and ponderosa pine forests, and river basins.

Comments

Related to medicinal ephedrine varieties but with a much milder effect. Can be useful as a decongestant, opening the lungs, and for allergy relief.

Tea is made from the branches. Used for medicinal purposes but can also be used as a beverage on a regular basis. Tea is high in calcium.

HORSETAIL
Equisetum arvense

Family: Equisetaceae
Other names: Field horsetail, common horsetail
Lookalikes: Scouring rush, Mormon tea
WARNING: Sources advise that large quantities can be toxic because of the enzyme thiaminase, which robs the body of vitamin B. Small quantities are fine. Cooking or drying removes thiaminase. Do not gather from heavily fertilized fields or ditches, as this species can concentrate nitrates and become toxic. Also can concentrate selenium when heavy in soils.

FORAGER NOTE: At certain stages of development horsetail can look like scouring rush (*E. hyemale*), but horsetail is distinguished by the whorled leaves protruding from the stem joints.

Description

Horsetail has two very distinct growth phases. In spring it sends out a fertile, unbranched shoot that somewhat resembles scouring rush, but it is light brown to brown and more fleshy and stout (thicker). It is 4"–6" tall and about ¼" wide. A spore-producing cone (which also resembles the scouring rush) tops the shoot before it withers away.

In late spring the perennial root systems send out infertile vegetative shoots. These green, jointed stems, ridged at the joints, grow to about 2' tall (sometimes taller). Smaller, similar looking branches emerge from the main stalks, creating the appearance of an emerging evergreen tree. Small, narrow leaves are whorled at stem joints.

Range and Habitat

Found from 2,900' in altitude in Montana up to 10,800' in Colorado. In other regions found down to sea level. Prefers moist sites in woods, fields, meadows, riverbanks, lakes, disturbed areas, and swamps. Also found in drier locations, such as roadsides. From Alaska to Texas and through much of the eastern United States.

Comments

Can be taken for short periods of time as a medicinal tea to strengthen connective tissue. Also used as a diuretic and for liver, kidney, and lung health.

RECIPE

Tea

Pour boiling water over a heaping teaspoon of horsetail. Steep covered, and drink three times per day. Take a break after a few weeks.

Variation: Make a mild decoction by boiling the herb in water for 5 to 15 minutes.

SCOURING RUSH
Equisetum hyemale

Family: Equisetaceae

Other names: Common scouring rush, scouringrush horsetail, horsetail, rough horsetail, scouring horsetail, tall scouring rush, western scouringrush, tall scouring rush, Dutch rush, *Hippochaete hyemalis*

Lookalikes: Bamboo, horsetail, Mormon tea

WARNING: Sources advise that large quantities can be toxic because the plant contains the enzyme thiaminase, which robs the body of vitamin B. Small quantities are fine. Cooking or drying removes thiaminase. Do not gather from heavily fertilized fields or ditches (fertilizer runoff), as this species can concentrate nitrates and become toxic. Also can concentrate selenium when selenium is heavy in soils.

FORAGER NOTE: At certain stages of development, scouring rush can look like horsetail (*E. arvense*) but unlike horsetail, scouring rush has no leaves.

Description

This perennial native looks like a smaller version of bamboo. Erect, straight, grass-like or bamboo-like stalks stand up to about 3' tall. Hollow, jointed and leafless. Periodic black and white bands encircle the stalk. Spreads by rhizomatous root systems and is usually found in large patches.

Spore cones, instead of flower heads, are dark yellow with black spots. Cones are about ¾" long.

Range and Habitat

Very moist locations from Alaska across the entire Rocky Mountain region to Florida. Moist forests, forest edges, and riparian areas. Can tolerate full submersion in water. Found up to about 9,840' in elevation.

Comments

Stems are covered in silica, which is good for teeth and bones. Blend a stalk in blender with your smoothie, or steep for tea. Often confused with its relative *Equisetum arvense,* also called horsetail. Many medicinal uses for liver, kidneys, and urinary tract ailments, as well as asthma.

Use dried bundles to scour and shine aluminum and copper and to polish wood. Provides food for geese and other waterfowl. Also good for scrubbing pots, pans, and teeth.

RECIPE

Homemade Toothpaste

A version of this recipe was shown to me by Katrina Blair, founder of the Turtle Lake Refuge, an inspirational wild foods restaurant and education center in Durango, Colorado. I have tried every natural toothpaste available in stores, and this one is by far the best.

A variety of clays are appropriate as a toothpaste ingredient. Ask someone at your local herbal store about what you can use for toothpaste.

Use crisp, dried scouring rush that has been dried in a dark place with good airflow. Blend in blender to a powder consistency.

Combine equal parts powdered scouring rush and clay with a few drops of essential mint oil. Add just enough water to make a very thick paste. Make enough to last for a week's worth of toothbrushing. Store in refrigerator for up to a week.

NODDING ONION
Allium cernuum

Family: Liliaceae

Other names: Wild onion, lady's leek

Lookalikes: Death camas (*Zigadenus venenosus;* **poisonous**), western blue flag (*Iris missouriensis;* **poisonous**)

Related species: Short-styled onion (*A. brevistylum*), taper tip onion (*A. acuminatum*), Geyer's onion (*A. geyeri*), prairie onion (*A. textile*)

WARNING: All wild onions can be confused with the toxic death camas. The basal leaf clusters look similar, but death camas flowers are quite different. They are conical-pyramidal clusters of cream or lavender flowers that are more tightly clustered than the onion flower heads. To be safe, identify wild onion for consumption only when flowers are present. Large quantities of death camas are suspected to cause poisoning of some mammals.

Leaves and young shoots also look like the wild iris, called western blue flag (*Iris missouriensis*). This species looks like a garden-variety iris but is much smaller. It grows in similar habitats as wild onion—moist, open meadows—so again, it's best to identify onion when flowers are present. Iris is NOT EDIBLE.

Description

This slender, delicate-looking native perennial has six to ten long, narrow, grass-like basal leaves that soar upwards to about 1' tall and ¼" wide around the leafless stalk. Leaves are generally shorter than the flower stalk. Nodding onion grows to about 1½' tall but is often smaller. It has an oniony scent. One flower stalk emerges from each underground bulb.

Flowers are pink, light pink, or white. Flower heads are loose clusters of three petals and three sepals with long yellow anther-topped white stamens. Blooms mid- to late summer.

Nodding onion is notable by the way the flower head and the top of the peduncle (main flower stem) nod downwards in an elegant rounded sweep. Also, each flower in the cluster sits atop a nodding pedicle (individual flower stem) that also rounds downward. Seeds are black.

Range and Habitat

From British Columbia to Texas and spottily around the country. Found in full or partial sun, open meadows, roadsides, from the plains to subalpine zone throughout the Rockies.

FORAGER NOTE: Death camas does not smell like onion, so use your sense of smell in identification. Wild onions smell distinctly like onions. However, beware that because onions are so pungent, if there are onions and death camas growing in the same location, your nose can be fooled.

Comments

All wild onions are edible. The bulb can be used like any onion—raw, dried, pickled, or cooked. Flowers and young shoots can also be eaten raw or cooked (but do not confuse shoots with death camas or iris shoots). Harvest is restricted in Arizona and some other states, so be sure to check your local listings before harvesting.

Be aware that harvesting the bulb kills the plant. Harvest only when there is a large cluster of onions growing together. I often see nodding onion growing singly or in small clusters of up to eight plants. In this case you can perhaps harvest a few leaves and a flower, but that is all that is acceptable.

RECIPE

Sautéed Shrimp and Onion with Brown Rice

Cook 1 cup short-grain brown rice in rice cooker. Chop enough onion to make 2 cups of large pieces. Slice 1½ tablespoons fresh ginger into strips.

Heat olive oil or bacon fat in a heavy skillet to medium-high heat. Sauté onion and ginger about 7 minutes. Add 12 shrimp. Sauté about 8 minutes, or until shrimp is done. Remove from heat, and place in a serving bowl.

Warm skillet again to medium and toss in 2 cups roughly chopped mizuna, chard, or other hardy green. Stir until wilted, about 4 minutes.

Place brown rice in bowl; top with Bragg's or soy sauce and a sprinkle of flax seeds. Add shrimp and greens. Serve hot.

RECIPE

Potato Crusted Onion Frittata

Preheat oven to 375°F. Coat the bottom of a 9 x 13" glass baking dish with olive oil. Slice several potatoes about ¼" thick, and line baking dish with one layer of potatoes. Some overlap is fine.

Add to baking dish on top of the potatoes: a layer of sliced tomatoes and a layer of broccoli or chopped kale, or a combination.

In a mixing bowl combine 4 farm-fresh eggs, ¼ cup homemade almond milk (or other milk), and 4 wild onion bulbs, chopped. (To prepare bulbs, peel outer layer off). Add plenty of salt and pepper.

Pour egg mixture over the vegetables. Bake until just firm and beginning to brown, about 40 to 60 minutes. With such dramatic variations in altitude in our region, baking times will vary. Adjust as needed.

Variation: Add grated cheese to the egg mixture; beat in well.

WESTERN BLUE FLAX
Linum lewisii

Family: Linaceae
Other names: Wild blue flax, blue flax, prairie flax, Lewis flax, *Linum perenne*
Lookalikes: Chicory
WARNING: Green seeds should not be eaten; eat only the mature dark seeds. Some sources warn that wild flax seeds **must be cooked** to remove cyanide compounds and that toxic reactions can occur if not properly prepared. Others believe they are perfectly safe to eat raw.

Description
This pretty native perennial flowers in spring and produces small edible flax seeds in late summer. Its erect, branching stems are 3"–36" tall. Small (up to 1⅓") leaves are alternate, linear, or lanceolate and closely hug the stem. Basal leaves can remain green year-round. Does not flower until third (sometimes second) year. Light purplish-blue flowers (rarely white) have five petals and are up to 2" wide.

Range and Habitat

Seen widely along roadsides; blooms in spring and early summer, going to seed by late summer. Ranges from Alaska to Texas in montane areas, roadsides, meadows, high mountain grasslands, and open fields up to about 9,100' in elevation. Early stage pioneer species, so often found in disturbed sites throughout the range.

Comments

Wild flax seeds are a little bit smaller than store-bought varieties. Seeds can be eaten raw, roasted, dried, or sprouted. But see warning above, as some sources say wild flax seeds should not be eaten raw.

I put flax seeds on just about everything from rice dishes to smoothies to salads, and I often include them in baked goods like cookies. They are somewhat gelatinous and help hold baked goods together in much the same way that eggs do. Eaten raw, they are pleasant and smooth.

RECIPE

Raw Pumpkin Pie with Flax and Nut Crust

Place 1 cup raw almonds or cashews (or a combination) and 1 cup fat, juicy raisins or dates (or a combination) in a food processor fitted with the metal blade. Blend briefly; add ¼ cup flax seeds and ½ teaspoon cinnamon. Blend very well, until all ingredients are finely chopped and begin to stick together like dough. Remove from food processor and press evenly into a pie plate.

Fill with raw pumpkin pie filling or raw fruit filling of your choice.

Harvest seeds in early fall. They fall out easily when the seed capsule is cracked and gently shaken. Seeds can be stored raw or roasted. Seeds can be eaten whole or ground. You can sprout them first and then eat them whole or ground. Many people prefer to eat flax seeds ground rather than whole to better assimilate nutrients into the body. It is best to store flax seed whole, however, to preserve oil quality.

This plant is related to common flax (*L. usitatissimum*), a European annual species that is cultivated for its seeds. Pollinated by flies, bees, and other insects.

High in omega-3 fatty acids and fiber. Gelatinous, so it makes a good gelling agent for recipes, lotions, and hair gel.

Strong fibers can be made into cord, baskets, nets, and webbing for snowshoes.

MALLOW
Malva neglecta

Family: Malavaceae
Other names: Common mallow, cheeseweed, cheese plant, button weed
Related species: Round-leaf mallow (*M. pusilla*), dwarf mallow (*M. rotundifolia*)

Description

This nonnative species of mallow is usually an annual but in some places is a perennial or biennial.

Mallow is decumbent (sometimes somewhat erect), with one or many branched stems and sprawling arms up to 3' long, depending on growing

RECIPE

Apple-Mallow Fruit Salad

Dice 1 apple into small 1" squares. Cover in fresh-squeezed juice of ½ lemon, and toss to prevent browning. Toss with ½ cup mallow peas. Serve at room temperature.

conditions. Its herbaceous stalks are up to ¼" thick. Leaves are palmate, alternate, and about 2½"–3" wide. The leaves are roundish or kidney shaped with five shallow lobes, toothed, and wavy. Leaves have a deep indent at the base where they attach to the long petioles (leaf stems). They somewhat resemble small hollyhock leaves and are covered in tiny, unnoticeable hairs.

Flowers are about ¾" wide, occur in groups of one to three, and are white, pinkish, violet, or white with pinkish stripes or markings.

The small fruits are round and light green, with a darker green-rimmed circle toward the center. These little buttons are sectioned and look like wheels of cheese. Fruits are ¼–½" in diameter and are halfway surrounded by the calyx, which looks like a delicate light-green leaf basket holding each fruit.

Range and Habitat
From British Columbia and throughout most of the United States, including Alaska. Mallow is a common garden weed found up to at least 8,900' in elevation.

Comments
Leaves and young shoots are edible raw or cooked. The young tender leaves are especially good in salad. The little fruits, or peas (cheese wheels), are incredible, and I'll admit to having a bit of an obsession.

To harvest the buttons, pluck the fruit from its calyx basket and eat as is, in a salad, or cooked. They are smooth and melt in your mouth. Flowers are edible raw but should be harvested and eaten soon after or they will wilt. Same with leaves, which can be soaked in water to prevent wilting. Mallow flower tea is also good. As mallow seeds age they turn brown and can be sprouted and eaten as any sprout.

Soak any part of the plant in water and the water will become gooey and mucilaginous. Use the gooey water as lotion. Add essential oils for extra home-spa yumminess.

For an absolutely extraordinary discussion of mallow, read *Edible Wild Plants* by John Kallas, PhD. John's experimentation with soaking mallow and using the mucilaginous water to make a wild but very civilized version of marshmallows and a perfectly fluffy, browned meringue pie topping is mind-blowing. It makes you want to shout, "The pie. Don't forget the pie." A must read.

RECIPE

Mallow Gumbo

Mallow is so much like okra, it just screams to be used in a traditional New Orleans–style Gumbo, especially since I almost never see any decent-looking okra being sold in stores in the Rocky Mountains (although it can be grown here quite successfully). Substitute young mallow leaves for okra in equal quantities in any gumbo recipe. The fruits can also be used, but I have a hard time preventing myself from eating them raw to save a sufficient quantity for anything else.

RECIPE

Raw Mallow Wheels

Harvest the fruits, and remove the leafy calyx that partially surrounds them. Serve raw in a small bowl with other light appetizers like olives, cheese, apple wedges, and crackers.

FIREWEEDS
Epilobium angustifolium

Family: Onagraceae

Other names: Common fireweed, perennial fireweed, narrow-leaved fireweed, great willow-herb, rosebay willow-herb, alpine fireweed, blooming sally, *Chamerion angustifolium*

Related species: Dwarf or broad-leaved fireweed (*E. latifolium*), a shorter relative

Description

Erect native perennial reaching 2'–8' tall with showy pink flowers. Smooth stems, mostly unbranched, green or sometimes reddish.

Leaves are narrow, hairless, lanceolate or linear, with smooth or lightly toothed margins and short petioles. They have a pronounced white midvein and grow to 2½"–5½" long. Leaves are long, narrow, and willow-like and very similar to the leaves of its relative, the evening primrose. Lots of alternate leaves along the stem form a spiral pattern.

Flowers form in a loose, elongated triangular raceme cluster along the top portion of the stalk. Very showy flowers are pink, magenta, or purplish (rarely white), each about 1" wide, with four petals and four sometimes-darker sepals. Flower clusters are about 8" long along the stalk and can bloom throughout summer. The entire raceme does not bloom at the same time, so it is common to see developing seedpods along with blooming flowers. Each flower produces 300 to 500 seeds, which travel by wind to reproduce.

Grows in dense clusters from hardy rhizomes that can extend 15"–17" deep into the soil and spread horizontally underground. Rhizomes survive after forest fires, making fireweed one of the early post-fire ecosystem recovery pioneers.

Range and Habitat

From Alaska across the West to New Mexico, all of Canada, and into the northeastern United States. Riparian areas in alpine, subalpine, and montane zones. Early pioneer after fires. Roadsides, pastures, riverbanks, burned forests, and rocky riverside outcrops.

RECIPE

Flower and Leaf Trail Salad

Harvest leaves and flowers. Eat right from the stalk, or bring along a bowl and toss leaves with a simple olive oil, vinegar, and salt and pepper dressing that you prepared at home. Beautiful, fresh, and healthy.

Steamed Young Shoots

Make note where the fireweed stand is, and go back in spring to harvest young shoots. Gently steam and top with butter and salt, or toss lightly with homemade pesto.

Comments

Edible parts include young shoots (raw or cooked), older stems (peeled, raw or cooked), leaves (raw, cooked, or dried and used for tea), roots (raw or roasted), and flowers (raw or as jelly or candy).

Many accounts say the older leaves are too bitter to eat. I do not find this to be true, although they sometimes give a somewhat prickly-hairy mouth feel that is not the most pleasant.

Dry old stalks can also be used to make cordage.

Eaten by moose, deer, caribou, muskrats, hares, and other wildlife. Taking some cuttings early in spring can stimulate additional growth, but this species is very sensitive to being trampled, so care should be taken not to step on fireweed stands.

EVENING PRIMROSE
Oenothera biennis

Family: Onagraceae
Other names: Common evening primrose
Lookalikes: Great mullein
WARNING: Can have a sedative effect for some. Take caution when driving, caring for children, etc., until you know how this plant treats you.

Description

Native biennial that forms a star-like rosette in its first year and sends up a stalk 2'–8' tall in spring of the second year. Leaves are narrow and linear, with a prominent light green or whitish colored midvein. Leaves alternate along a stalk about 6" long.

Thick, sturdy, erect stalks occasionally branch once or twice.

Yellow, four-petaled flowers form tight clusters along the top portion of the stalk. Open in afternoon and evening. Fruits are hairy, tubular seedpods that point upward from the stalk, for a short time with the remains of the flowers sticking out of their tops.

Boiled Root and Leaves with Winter Stew

Harvest roots of several basal rosettes after the first hard frost. Scrub well. Cut into large chunks about 2" to 3" long. Bring large pot of salted water to a boil. Add primrose roots. Boil for about 15 minutes; drain and change water. Bring a new pot of salted water to a moderate boil, and boil again for 15 minutes; drain, rinse, and set aside.

In the now-empty large pot, heat olive oil. Add 1 cup roughly chopped onion and 5 cloves garlic, chopped. Sauté with 4 cups wild game or beef (stew cuts are fine) cut into 2" to 3" chunks, until browned but not cooked through.

Add the boiled roots and 1 cup primrose leaves. Add a few cups chicken or veggie broth, enough to cover the meat and roots. Add 3 bay leaves and 2 carrots, roughly chopped. Bring to a boil then reduce heat and simmer with a cracked lid for 30 to 60 minutes, stirring occasionally. Make sure the meat is cooked through.

Serve hot over rice, with fresh crusty bread or a side salad.

Smoothie Topped with Primrose Seeds

This is one of my favorites, and come fall I seem to constantly crave it. The recipe is very simple.

Fill a blender container halfway with orange juice. Add 1 organic banana, 2 small handpicked apples (seeds and core removed), 6 ice cubes, and a pinch each turmeric and ginger (or fresh ginger root). Blend well on high speed until ice is pulverized. Pour into pint glasses, and top with a pinch cinnamon and ½ teaspoonful of primrose seeds. Enjoy.

Roots are whitish; their size depends on how compact the soil is and how much moisture was present.

Range and Habitat
British Columbia to Texas. Moderately dry roadsides and fields up to about 9,000' in elevation.

Comments
Roots are eaten raw or cooked. Can be roasted, fried, boiled, dried, or sautéed. Some people advise boiling roots more than an hour and changing water at least once to improve flavor.

Flowers, flower buds, and leaves can be eaten raw or cooked. Roots are best harvested from the first year basal rosette during fall, winter, or early spring before the stalk emerges.

Raw seeds are high in linoleic acid and gamma linoleic acid and make a good omega-3 supplement.

NOTE: The hairy-throat feeling left by the leaves and roots can be unpleasant.

COMMON PLANTAIN
Plantago major

Family: Plantaginaceae

Other names: Ribwort, broadleaf plantain, buckhorn plantain, rippleseed plantain, greater plantain, white man's footprint

WARNING: Do not confuse plantain leaves with those of young hellebore, which is poisonous.

Description

Simple, roundish green leaves are low-growing basal rosettes and notable by the prominent ribs on their undersides. Leaves grow to about 6" long and 4" wide and lie more or less horizontally along the ground (sometimes they pop up a bit).

This nonnative, perennial herb produces a light brown, leafless flower stalk 3"–16" high. Tiny yellowish or greenish flowers tightly hug the stalk and bloom

> FORAGER NOTE: This plant shares a common name with the tropical banana-like fruit, also called plantain. They are not related and do not look alike at all.

throughout summer and into fall. Seeds ripen from midsummer to fall. All parts are mucilaginous.

Range and Habitat

From Alaska to Texas and across the United States in disturbed areas and lawns and along roadsides. Found in the plains and foothills throughout the Rockies in both dry and moist areas. A common plant found around the planet, including gardens, banks of ponds, and clearings.

RECIPE

Poultice for Insect Bites

Crush several clean leaves by chewing them gently between the teeth. Place directly onto welt caused by an insect bite. Hold in place until pain and swelling subside. Depending on the severity, you may want to replace with a fresh poultice after a while. If you are treating someone else, you may choose to crush the leaves in your hands to make the poultice or have the patient chew the leaves. **NOTE:** This is *not* a remedy for poison-infused bites, such as those from a venomous spider.

RECIPE

Herb Infused Olive Oil with Steamed Plantain Salad

For the oil: This works especially well if you have an herb garden. Harvest tarragon from your garden. Wash and pat dry. Allow to dry (just the water from rinsing it, not the entire herb). Place ¼ cup fresh herbs in a ½-quart jar, and fill with good quality olive oil. Do not pack tightly; leave plenty of room for the oil. Place in the back of your cupboard and allow to infuse for 1 to 2 weeks. Strain herb out and retain oil.

   For the salad: Harvest plantain leaves and remove the tough mid-vein. Chop into strips and steam until the leaves turn darker green and collapse. Remove from heat, and place in serving bowl atop fresh lettuce greens. Sprinkle with infused oil and a touch of sea salt. Sprinkle with seeds of the plantain if they are in season. Otherwise, flax or sunflower seeds are a nice alternative.

Comments

Leaves, stalks, and seeds are edible. Leaves can be eaten as any leafy green vegetable. Young leaves, and those not exposed to harsh conditions like excessive drought are tenderer. It can help palatability to remove the very fibrous mid-vein and other ribs from the leaf.

   Seeds can be eaten raw or cooked (often boiled). Young flower stalks can also be eaten like green beans.

   These small plants often go unnoticed as just another common weed. I have heard that chewing plantain leaves can be effective in creating an aversion to smoking tobacco. Use as a cold infused tea or poultice. Seeds have fiber and can be used as a supplement and a laxative or, like psyllium, for intestinal health. Plantain is astringent, antimicrobial and anti-inflammatory. Leaves can be used as a poultice for insect bites and poison ivy.

PURSLANE
Portulaca oleracea

Family: Portulacaceae

Other names: Common purslane, pursley, wild or common portulaca, pusley, pigweed (although amaranth is more commonly referred to as pigweed)

WARNING: Purslane has been reported to contain dangerous levels of oxalates, which can cause problems for livestock and humans. Most foragers consider it an excellent source of nutrition and have no problem with consuming reasonable quantities.

Description

This prostrate (flat-growing) succulent ground cover has smooth, thick, reddish stems and smooth leaves that are often nearly opposite. Leaves appear in whorls or clusters at the stem joints and tips. Leaves do not reach much more than 1" long but together form a thick and spreading ground cover. Small, solitary, yellow flowers bloom from stem ends but are very short-lived and rarely seen.

Purslane's taproot is fibrous and branching, making it well suited to drought conditions. Its tiny black seeds form within a little nest, visible when the short-lived flower falls away.

Range and Habitat

Common garden weed from British Columbia through the Rocky Mountain region to Florida. Found in gardens, lawns, and disturbed areas. An old-world native, there is some debate about whether there was a pre-Columbian species in our hemisphere. Purslane is a hot-weather plant that sprouts in midsummer once the soil has warmed.

Comments

Leaves, stems, and seeds are edible raw, pickled (like sauerkraut), or cooked. Purslane can also be dried, but because it is fat and juicy, drying is not most people's preferred method.

Because purslane is so low growing, it is usually quite covered in dirt. It is such a sturdy plant, though, that cleaning is easy. Soak in a few changes of water, disturbing it to release the soil, or rinse using a colander.

Purslane has a strong sour-lemony taste and goes well with other flavorful foods. Spanish speakers of the Southwest called pickled purslane *chao chao*. It can be made with peppers, zucchini, and onions.

This is such a common weed that you just cross your fingers and hope it is edible. It certainly is, and purslane doesn't disappoint. As Katrina Blair, told me, "It is delicious. A true wild food delicacy; juicy, slightly sour and mild. It is agreeable to most people's palate."

Purslane has an extraordinary amount of omega-3 fatty acids and is a great substitute for fish oil supplements, which can be high in heavy metals. Purslane is also high in vitamin E and other nutrients. An important component of the Mediterranean diet, purslane has been an important staple and ceremonial food crop around the world for thousands of years. It is also a great companion plant for breaking up soil, as its roots dig deep into hard-packed ground, and as ground cover to retain moisture. Think twice before pulling purslane as a weed.

RECIPE

Raw Purslane Salad

Chop 1 small red onion, 1 cup purslane leaves and stems, 1 peeled cucumber, and 2 large garden-fresh tomatoes. Combine in a bowl; toss with 1 tablespoon each olive oil and rice vinegar. Add fresh-ground black pepper and a splash of tamari; toss well. Let sit in a cool place or at room temperature for 15 to 20 minutes. Add raw sesame seeds; toss and serve.

Variation: Add ½ teaspoon honey to the dressing. Prepare the oil, vinegar, tamari, pepper, and honey in a separate bowl; mix well. Toss with the salad.

Good Old-Fashioned Sausage, Onion, and Purslane

Grill 4 links spicy sausage and slice into bite-size pieces. Slice and then sauté 1 medium to large yellow onion in olive oil in a skillet. When onion is halfway to caramelized, add 1 cup chopped purslane. Continue to sauté until almost caramelized. Toss with sausage; serve on a bed of brown rice. Garnish with garden-fresh parsley.

Instead allow it to benefit your garden and provide essential fatty acids and other nutrients to your diet.

The uses for purslane are endless. Its gooey quality helps thicken soups and stews and can be used like okra for this purpose, although the taste is more pronounced than okra. Purslane can also be used in drinks where thickness and a lemon flavor are desired.

WILD STRAWBERRY
Fragaria spp.

Family: Rosaceae
Other names: Thick-leaved wild strawberry
Lookalikes: Cinquefoil (leaves)
Related species: Woodland strawberry (*F. vesca*), Virginia strawberry (*F. virginiana*)

Description
More than twenty species worldwide, with many more subspecies and cultivars. All look similar, with some differences in leaf and fruit size and variations in geographic range and habitat.

Leaves sometimes look like a single leaf with three deep, sharply serrated lobes. Other leaves are more like three separate leaflets coming out of a single point at the tip of the leaf stalk. Leaves grow up to about 4" long and are always toothed, sometimes waxy, sometimes not. Leaves turn colorful in fall and make a pretty red-hued ground cover. Leaves are somewhat similar to the leaves of cinquefoil but almost always less accordion pleated.

Flower petals are short and fat (rounded with a slight tip) and white. Inflorescence are clustered, a few together, and have a prominent bright yellow center.

Strawberry plants are low growing (up to 1' high) and spreading. They produce a basal rosette of coarsely serrated three-lobed leaves. Plants send out long runners that set root in the soil. Strawberries are not really fruits but are commonly referred to as a fruit or berry. The berries are bright red and much smaller

than store-bought varieties, usually less than 1". Achenes housing the seeds dot the outside of the berries. Depending on the species, achenes might protrude or be deeply seated in the red flesh.

Range and Habitat
Found throughout the entire continent. Large spreading mats on forest floors and in dappled shade, especially where somewhat moist.

Comments
Wild strawberries are small and often sparse. It's usually irresistible to eat the few that you can find straight from the plant. If some do manage to make it home with you, they make a great addition to desserts (decorate a cake or cookie platter), cereal, drinks, and salads.

RECIPE

Fresh Fruit Muesli

Combine 1 cup organic oats, ¾ cup rye flakes, ¼ cup dried cherries or raisins (unsweetened, unsulfured), ¼ cup pumpkin seeds, ¼ cup crushed or slivered almonds, ⅛ cup sunflowers seeds, ⅛ cup flax seeds. Serve in a bowl with homemade almond milk or vanilla yogurt, and top with plenty of fresh wild strawberries.

   Variation: Add additional fresh fruit like blueberries, plums, and apples.

NORTHERN BEDSTRAW
Galium boreale

Family: Rubiaceae
Other names: Cleavers, *G. septentrionale*
Related species: Sweet-scented bedstraw (*G. triflorum*), three-petal bedstraw (*G. trifidum*), cleavers (*G. aparaine*)

Description
This delicate looking native perennial is recognizable by its distinct, narrow leaves (lanceolate or linear) that form along the smooth stalk in whorls of four. Leaves are up to about 2" long, with some whorls of smaller leaves. Stalks grow 1'–3' tall. Other species of bedstraw have more rounded, wider leaves.

Showy, dense clusters of tiny whitish flowers bloom in spring. Northern bedstraw reproduces by seed and creeping rhizomatic root systems. Seed clusters look almost like flowers from a slight distance. They are rounded pink to cream capsules.

G. aparine is a very common species. It is a naturalized nonnative annual, whereas most bedstraws are perennial.

Range and Habitat

From Alaska to New Mexico in foothills, on montane slopes, and in moist meadows or woods. Also found west to California and across the northeastern United States and all of Canada.

Comments

All species are interchangeable in edibility and uses. Seeds and roots can be roasted and used like coffee. Bedstraw leaves are a potherb and can be added to any soup or stew for extra nutrition, although they are fairly bland tasting. Leaves are small, so it does take some time to collect a sufficient amount. The thin graceful leaves are nice as a garnish.

Used as food and as medicine against tumors and inflammation. The leaves of some species can be unpleasant raw; their hairiness can upset the throat and mouth. Boiled, they are perfectly enjoyable.

RECIPE

Baked Cleaver Lasagna (gluten free)

Preheat oven to 400°F. Cover the bottom of a heavy baking dish (with a lid) with 1–2 tablespoons olive oil. Next sprinkle 4 cloves garlic, chopped, over the oil; sprinkle 1 teaspoon salt evenly around.

Slice two yellow summer squash into ¼"–½" thick slices. Arrange in a layer, laid like lasagna noodles on the bottom of the baking dish.

Next add a layer of bedstraw leaves, approximately ½ cup. Spread leaves out evenly across the squash layer. Sprinkle 1 teaspoon truffle oil (optional) over the leaves. Add layer of mozzarella cheese (about ½ cup) or cheese substitute. Sprinkle with salt and pepper. Add a layer of sliced zucchini from 1 medium-size zucchini. Top with 1 cup mozzarella cheese or cheese substitute, ⅛ teaspoon fresh-ground black pepper, and ¼ teaspoon paprika.

Bake, covered, for 30 minutes. Rotate pan and remove lid. Continue cooking 15 to 25 minutes more, until bubbling and cheese begins to brown.

RECIPE

Fresh Trout with Bedstraw Garnish

In a bowl combine ½ cup coarse cornmeal, 1 tablespoon large-grain sea salt, 1 tablespoon fresh-ground black pepper, and 1 teaspoon cayenne powder. Mix well to combine.

Dunk 4 medium-size, moist trout fillets, one at a time, into the cornmeal mixture. Rotate bowl, and cover all sides of the filet with as much cornmeal as possible. Use your hands to gently press cornmeal mixture into fish.

In a small saucepan bring 3 cups water to a boil. Add 1 cup bedstraw leaves. Boil for 5 minutes and drain. Toss leaves in a bowl with the juice of 1 lemon and set aside.

Heat 4 tablespoons canola oil in a skillet to medium high. When a drop of water sizzles on the oil, add the fish. Cook until just browned on bottom; flip, and brown the other side. Remove from heat and place on plates. Garnish with the bedstraw leaves, gently laying the leaves out in a crisscross pattern across the top of the fish. Garnish with a lemon wedge. Serve atop of a bed of mixed greens.

GREAT MULLEIN
Verbascum thapsus

Family: Scrophulariaceae
Other names: Common mullein, lungwort, velvet dock, velvet plant, punchon, gordolobo, candlewick
Lookalikes: Evening primrose (*Oenothera biennis*)
WARNING: The **seeds are toxic** and should not be eaten. Do not confuse flower buds with seeds. Seeds are also toxic to fish so should not be thrown into waterways. The hairs on the leaves are rubefacient, or irritating to the skin.

Tea made with the flowers can be a mild sedative, so experiment with small amounts first. When making tea, be sure to strain it well to remove the fine hairs, which can cause significant irritation. The leaves contain rotenone (an insecticide) and coumarin (prevents blood clotting) but are not problematic when used in normal quantities.

Description
This nonnative Eurasian immigrant is a biennial with thick, soft, rounded ovular leaves. In the first year the plant creates a basal rosette of large, thick, gray-green, felt-covered, rounded leaves. Leaves are covered in dense soft hairs, giving it the look and feel of velvet, similar to lamb's-ear.

In the second year the plant sends up a large straight stalk, sometimes branched a few times, that produces a dense cone of yellow flowers along the stalk. Flowers, flower buds, and seedpods are packed together and densely cover the stalk. Flowers open and go to seed at different times, even on the same stalk.

Mullein stalks are thick, about 2" in diameter, and grow from 1"–8" tall. Note that in some climates and conditions, mullein can be an annual or a short-lived perennial.

Range and Habitat

From Alaska south across the entire United States, including Hawaii. Mullein grows in sunny, disturbed areas; along roadsides; and in vacant lots and open fields. Found from sea level to tree line.

Comments

Many people consider great mullein medicinal only. Others consider it edible.

Flower buds and flowers are edible raw, cooked, or dried. Flower buds make a wonderful trail snack. They are tender and sweet. **Caution:** Do not confuse with the poisonous seedpods, which can often be found right next to emerging buds.

Leaves are generally washed, dried, and used as medicinal tea. The roots also can also be used for medicinal teas. Dried leaves

RECIPE

Mullein Flower Tea

Yellow mullein flowers are a great substitute to prepackaged tea. Boil hot water, and steep a spoonful of flowers, covered, for 5 to 10 minutes. **NOTE:** Filter thought cheesecloth to remove irritating fine hairs.

    Variation: Add fresh rose hips or wild rose petals.

can be smoked medicinally, though some find this use questionable.

The fine hairs on all parts of the plant cause irritation in the throat and mouth and need to be strained out through a cheesecloth or fine sieve.

Be careful when picking flower buds. **Do not confuse flower buds with seedpods.** It is easy to do. **The seeds are poisonous.** The flowers bloom and go to seed at different times on the same stalk, so confusion is very possible.

My favorite way to use great mullein is as a blush. Harvest one leaf and rub gently on the apple of the cheek for a healthy glow.

Mullein is also called lungwort because it is used as a medicinal herb for hay fever and asthma, to reduce inflammation in lungs, and for ear infections.

The soft, thick, velvety leaves can be used as liners for shoes, toilet paper (directionality is everything), or menstrual pads. Flowers can be made into a hair dye. Mullein can be used as a poultice to reduce swelling, to help heal sprains, and as an expectorant. The plant also contains vitamins B2, B5, B12, and D; choline; hesperidin; para-aminobenzoic acid; magnesium; and sulfur.

RECIPE

Great Mullein Torch

Great mullein can be dipped in suet or wax and used as a torch. Melt candle wax, and dip the mullein stalk several times to create multiple wax layers. Let dry in between layers. Take care with open flame, and *never* leave unattended or burn where there is risk of starting a fire.

CATTAILS
Typha latifolia

Family: Typhaceae

Other names: Common cattail, broadleaf cattail

Lookalikes: Young shoots may resemble poisonous death camas, western blue flag, or other nonedible iris family members.

Related species: Narrowleaf cattail (*T. angustifolia*), which is very similar, but a small gap of less than 1"–4" separates the female and male portions of the flower along the flower stalk. The narrow-leaved variety grows slightly shorter, 3½'–5' tall, and the leaves are about ¼" wide.

WARNING: Some sources report that cattail should be avoided during pregnancy; others do not. Cattails are filter plants, and if they are growing in contaminated water or where there is contaminated runoff, they should NOT be consumed by anyone.

Description

Tall, narrow-leaved perennials growing in dense stands. An easy one to identify by the large, dark brown "hot dog on a stick" appearance of the flowers. Tall flower stalks are interspersed among the tall, straight green leaves. Plants reach 3'–9' in height. Erect, stiff leaves are tall and loosely surround the stalk; they are less than 1" wide.

Flowers are deceivingly un-flower-like, since the flowers do not have petals. Female flowers grow in dense bunches toward the top of the stalks and form a dense brown tube, or spike. Just above the female portion, at the tip of the stalk, are the male flowers, which are yellow and form a much thinner tube up to the pointed tip of the stalk. They are short-lived. It is the female portion of the flower that gives cattails their distinct appearance.

The flower spikes are less noticeable when they are young and still green. As they age they become brown and eventually float away like the cotton-like seedpods of dandelion or thistle.

Range and Habitat

Cattails grow in swamps, marshes, and calm, moist riparian zones from Canada to New Mexico. They are widespread in moist areas throughout the United States but not generally found in the higher elevations of the Rocky Mountains. They are often found in roadside drainages and pristine riparian areas throughout the region.

Comments

Cattails are highly edible and nutritious. The young flower spikes (green buds before they turn brown), corms (swollen tuber, bulb), rhizomes (thick lateral roots), lower portion of the leaves, peeled stalk, pollen, and seeds are edible.

RECIPE

Pollen Pancakes

Harvest yellow pollen from the male flowers by shaking it into a container or bag. There is no need to cut down the cattail in order to do this. There is a lot of pollen, so it is fairly simple to gather enough for a batch of pancakes. Substitute ¼ of the flour or pancake mix with pollen, and proceed as usual. Don't over sweeten with maple syrup or you will drown out the flavor of the pollen.

   WARNING: People with allergies to other pollens should be careful and try only a very small amount at first.

RECIPE

Grilled Cattail on the Cob

Harvest young, green female flower spikes. Place on grill over medium heat. Rotate so that no side becomes burned. Cook until the spikes just begin to brown; remove from heat. Eat like corn on the cob, plain or with butter and salt.

Variation: Instead of butter and salt, douse with fresh-squeezed lime juice, home-made mayonnaise, and top with roasted chili powder.

To eat the tender lower portion of the leaves, grasp the leaf at the base and pull it free. Scrape the flesh off with your teeth, or chop and add to salad.

The young shoots are a delicious and tender vegetable and can be used like asparagus or bamboo. Peel the outer layers and then boil, steam, or sauté the inner part of the stalk or eat raw.

Young green flower spikes can be grilled or boiled much like corn on the cob. Pollen can be shaken from the male flower spikes and used as a nutritious addition to pancakes and baked goods or as a roux to thicken stew.

The roots are also edible but quite fibrous. They are prepared by forcibly separating the fiber strands from the starchy root. Since cattails are perennials, harvesting the root will kill the plant, so be sure to harvest roots only from robust stands where there will be plenty of cattails left.

Old-timers dipped the flower stalk in bear fat to make lanterns. I've also been told that you can burn the brown part off as a way of winnowing the seeds, which can also be used as food. The stiff leaves of cattails can be used to weave baskets, floor mats, seats, and water-storage containers. The fluffy down from the seedpods can be used as stuffing for pillows, mattresses, and supposedly even for life jackets.

STINGING NETTLE
Urtica dioica

Family: Urticaceae
Other names: California nettle, slender nettle, tall nettle
Lookalikes: All members of the mint family also have square stems.
WARNING: Stings; can cause rash, hives, and allergic reactions. Harvest wearing gloves and a long-sleeved shirt. Can cause uterine contractions, so pregnant women should avoid contact. Some warn that the plant should not be consumed after it begins to seed because chemistry changes make it unsafe to consume. Older leaves can irritate the kidneys. Also, can interfere with allopathic drugs used for such ailments as diabetes and hypertension. Should not be used in combination with alcohol.

Description
This nonnative perennial has long, thin, deeply serrated, hairy, ovular or lance-shaped leaves with pointed tips. Leaves are simple and opposite and often hang downward. The undersides of the leaves have hollow, needle-like hairs. The hairs contain a toxin that stings and can cause a rash and hives, which usually dissipate within a day.

Thick, erect, square stalks are hairy and 1½"–10' tall, usually 3'–4' high. Stalks are up to 1" thick.

Small whitish, greenish, or pinkish flowers have sepals but no petals and cluster in spikes along the stalk in clusters about 4" long. The plant becomes thickly laden with green, narrow, drooping clusters of seedpods that hang off the stem.

Range and Habitat

From Alaska to Florida. Moist fields, moist disturbed ground, open woods, and rocky areas in the plains, foothills, and montane zone. Grows in dense, sporadic patches.

Comments

Young shoots, young leaves, and the root are edible. Cooking or drying eliminates the sting of the toxin and actually turns stinging nettle into a delicious and versatile vegetable. The young shoots and leaves are particularly tender before the plant flowers, but leaves can also be collected after first flowering. Can be cooked like any vegetable.

I have also heard that the roots can be eaten cooked like a potato, but I have not confirmed it. Tea can also be made and drunk fresh brewed or fermented.

Fibers can be used to make fine textiles or rope. Roots, seeds, and greens are used for medicinal purposes. Use leaves to make a cleansing tea along with other greens or dried as a nutritional supplement.

On a climbing trip to Wyoming, I pointed out a patch of stinging nettle. My friend the Wild Walker immediately helped confirm the identification by thrashing his thick bare arm about in the nettle patch. The red welts, itching, and hives that persisted until the end of the day proved that this plant was indeed stinging nettle.

VIOLETS
Viola spp.

Family: Violaceae

Related species: Western dog violet/early blue violets (*V. adunca*), Canada violet (*V. canadensis*), round-leaved yellow violet (*V. orbiculata*), yellow montane violet/yellow prairie violet (*V. nuttallii*)

Description

Violets are low growing and can be annual or perennial. The leaves are usually in a basal cluster but can be alternate along the short stalks. The classic leaf shape is heart shaped, but some varieties are more lanceolate or linear.

Showy flowers are purple, white, or yellow depending on species. They have five petals, with two matching petals pointing upwards, two petals that point one to each side or somewhat downwards, and a single bottom petal that is somewhat bulged and points down. The single petal is often notable by the purple, brown, blackish, or

pink stripes emanating out and down from the flower's center. These markings might also extend from the side petals. The flower head is usually open and showy.

Range and Habitat
Throughout the United States, but specific ranges vary depending on species. Found in moist dappled shade, dry meadows, gardens, and, for some species, up to subalpine zone.

Comments
These pretty flowers are considered a weed by some, an ornamental by others, and a special treat by foragers. All violets are edible. Leaves and flowers can be eaten raw or cooked or drunk as a tea. Flowers can be made into candy and wine.

RECIPE

Fresh Violet Salad

Harvest fresh leaves and flowers in spring or summer. If you can find several violet varieties (yellow and purple), even better. Toss delicate salad greens, such as butter lettuce, and violet greens with a light crisp olive oil and a good plum vinegar. Lightly salt and pepper. Top with violet flowers, making a pretty pattern of bright yellow and purple. This is an astonishingly gorgeous way to eat your greens.

Shrubs

SMOOTH SUMAC
Rhus glabra

Family: Anacardiaceae

Lookalikes: Poison sumac (*Rhus vernix;* **not edible**), staghorn sumac (hairy branches, edible)

WARNING: Looks similar to poison sumac, which can cause allergic reactions, irritation of the mucus membranes, and death. If inhaled, severe respiratory problems can result. Poison sumac basically grows in the eastern United States, but you should still be very careful in case it somehow manages to make it to the Rockies.

Bark, shoots, and root might be toxic. Sources are conflicting.

FORAGER NOTE: Distinguish the edible species of sumac from poison sumac by the location of the flowers. In poison sumac, conical flowers or drupe clusters hang from stems that emerge from the connection point between the leaf petiole (leaf stem) and the main branch. This is the corner where the leaf grows out of the branch. Edible species have flowers and drupe clusters that stand erect directly from the tips of the branches. Poison sumac has seven to thirteen smooth-edged leaflets per leaf stem.

Description

Native perennial shrub or small tree with erect, cone-shaped greenish or cream-colored flower clusters that become rust colored or red as they fruit and turn to seed. Fruits are somewhat sticky drupes that stand erect on the ends of smooth branches for edible varieties. Drupes are rounded but somewhat flattened.

Sumac can be low-lying ground cover or up to 9' tall. It can form thickets by spreading root systems. Hairless stems and branches are covered in a whitish wax-like coating.

Leaves are alternate and pinnately compound. Leaflets are unlobed, sharply serrate, and oblong or lanceolate. Leaflets are arranged in opposite pairs, with one lone leaflet at the tip of each leaf stem. They form an organized and distinct pattern of eleven to thirty-one leaflets per leaf stem. They taper to a pointed end and turn vibrantly colorful in the fall. Leaves are darker on top and lighter on the underside.

Range and Habitat

Widely from British Columbia across the entire United States. Grows in open woods, canyons, meadows, and waste places and on dry, rocky hillsides. Largest in rich, moist soils.

Comments

Fruits, leaf, stem, and oils are edible. Most often the fruit is made into a beverage. Fruit is somewhat lemony flavored and can be eaten raw or cooked. This is a common shrub and is excellent for making juice throughout much of the year. Seeds remain erect on the branches much of the year, often to spring, and can be used year-round.

RECIPE

Sumac Juice

In a bowl combine 1 cup sumac fruit/seeds with 2 cups cold water. Smash and pinch together with your hands to release the seeds from the dry flesh. Allow to sit for 15 minutes—longer for stronger flavored juice. Strain through a fine colander to remove seeds. Serve room temperature or cold, as you would lemonade.

THREE-LEAVED SUMAC/SKUNKBUSH
Rhus trilobata

Family: Anacardiaceae
Other names: Squawberry, squawbush, lemonade sumac, stinking sumac, ill-scented sumac, quailbush, basketbush, three-lobed sumac, lemita, polecat bush, *R. aromatica* var. *trilobata*
Lookalikes: Rocky mountain maple, currant, gooseberry
WARNING: Some people are allergic, especially those with extra sensitivity to poison ivy.

Description
This pungent, erect to spreading native shrub grows from 2'–12' tall and can form thickets 30' wide. Average height is around 4' tall. Arching, hairy branches form rounded thickets. Roots are branched and spreading.

Compound leaves are deeply three-lobed, often looking more like three separate leaflets that taper to points where they attach to the petiole (leaf stem). Leaves are alternate, with rounded teeth. Leaves and branches can smell like skunk but not in an unpleasant way, especially when crushed.

Bright-red berrylike drupes are ¼"–½" in diameter, often with sticky hairs.

Skunkbush Lemonade

Combine 2 cups fruits with 8 cups cold or room-temperature water. With your hands, mash the berries separating the fruits from the seeds. Soak for 3 to 12 hours. Stir or shake vigorously several times during the soaking period. Strain to remove seeds and skin. Serve cold like lemonade.

Variation: Add sugar or honey; blend well. Add several sprigs of mint.

Range and Habitat

From Alberta and Saskatchewan to Colorado, Texas and California in foothills, canyons, and dry rocky slopes from about 2,500'–7,500' in elevation.

Comments

Fruits and seeds can be eaten raw, cooked, or dried. Mix fruits with cornmeal to make cakes, or make fruits into jam. Dried fruits often hang onto branches throughout fall and winter, making them an important survival food for critters. Young branches can be woven into baskets and containers.

Clusters of berries dry on the branches and make a great trail snack well after summer has ended. Somewhat lemony flavored but in a smooth and refreshing rather than puckery way.

Squawberry Tapioca Pudding

Boil 1 cup berries in 3 cups water for 15 minutes. Mash fruits and strain through a fine colander, or Foley mill, collecting the juice in a bowl below.

Prepare tapioca pudding following package instructions. Use the squawberry juice instead of water or milk.

Serve warm or cold. Sprinkle a few raw berries on top for garnish.

COMMON RABBITBRUSH
Ericameria spp.

Family: Asteraceae

Other names: Golden rabbitbrush, chamisa chamiso

Related species: Rubber rabbitbrush/gray rabbitbrush (*E. nauseosa, Chrysothamnus nauseosus*), Parry's rabbitbrush (*E. parryi*), green rabbitbrush (*E. viscidiflorus*)

 All were formerly considered part of the *Chrysothamnus* genus but are now classified as *Ericameria*.

Lookalikes: Big sagebrush (from afar)

Description

This sweet-smelling native perennial shrub grows rapidly up to 7' tall (sometimes 10') and about 7' wide. Woody lower branches with branched greener to gray upper branches. Green rabbitbrush (*C. viscidiflorus*) is somewhat shorter, reaching only about 4' in height.

 Wide, rounded crowns flower in late summer to fall and are covered in prolific arrays of small yellow flowers.

Leaves are linear and tiny (about ⅟₂₅"). Foliage is green to grayish and varies within the species. *E. nauseosa* is distinguished by the white felt-like covering on its branches and leaves that helps prevent water loss and makes this a highly successful arid region plant.

Range and Habitat

From Montana and North Dakota throughout the Rockies and Four Corners states to Texas. Disturbed areas and open meadows in semi-desert and montane sites up to about 10,800' in elevation.

Very common along moderate-elevation roadsides throughout the region. Does fine in high-wind conditions. In fact, I could barely get an adequate photo of rabbitbrush, as it always seemed incredibly windy whenever I came upon the plant, usually along open roadsides from New Mexico to Wyoming.

Comments

Chew raw bark or leaves like chewing gum (far more fun than you might expect). Flowers can be used to make sun tea or hot tea.

Rabbitbrush has a variety of medicinal uses, and a medicinal tea of flowers and leaves can be used internally or externally. Flowers can be used to make a yellow dye, and boughs can also be used as a natural building material for outdoor structures, such as ceilings for sweat lodges and floors for cabins.

What I love about this plant is that it is so big and prolific; you can harvest several branches from any member of the species without harming the plant or the stand. It also reproduces readily from seed.

RECIPE

Rabbitbrush and Artemesia Soak

Ritual bathing and aromatic soaks are wonderful things to cultivate in our hectic modern lives. The American understanding of aromatherapy has become confused as factory-produced chemical scents are increasingly sold as aromatherapy. Develop your understanding of real aromatherapy, and of bathing rituals that help your body and mind feel nourished and able to succeed, using real plants.

Harvest several branches of rabbitbrush with fresh yellow flowers. Also harvest several stalks of one of the artemesia varieties. You can use big sagebrush or a less-woody variety like fringed or white sage. Place several boughs of each into the bathtub, and fill with hot water. Keep the bathroom door closed while the tub is filling to retain the aromatherapy. Turn the lights down low, and sink into your very own desert-scented spa. As you soak you can use the boughs to gently scrub and exfoliate your skin.

OREGON GRAPES
Mahonia repens

Family: Berberidaceae
Other names: Creeping Oregon grape, barberry, creeping mahonia, creeping barberry
Lookalikes: Holly
Related species: Tall Oregon grape/Tall mahonia/Holly-leaved barberry/Oregon holly grape (*M. aquifolium*)
WARNING: Roots are medicine and should be avoided during pregnancy, while breast-feeding, and if you have an overactive thyroid. They contain high doses of berberine, which can cause vomiting, kidney infection, and other medical problems.

Description

Native perennial shrubs or sub-shrubs. The wild mahonias can be tall (*M. aquifolium*) or low-lying (*M. repens*). Creeping mahonia (*M. repens*) forms low-lying, spreading clusters 4"–12" tall. Tall mahonia grows 1'–10' in height.

FORAGER NOTE: Though sometimes called barberry, this plant should not be confused with the many species of shrubs also called barberry, which are in the *Berberis* genus. Also not bearberry/kinnikinnick (*uva ursi*).

Leaves are green or blue-green, stiff, leathery, and waxy. This shrub is considered an evergreen, but the leaves turn reddish as they age and in fall and winter create a sturdy, colorful ground cover. Leaves are pinnately compound, with five to eleven opposite, oval-shaped leaflets per leaf stem and one single leaflet at the tip of each leaf stem. Leaflets have spiny looking teeth spaced out along the leaf edges.

Dense clusters of yellow flowers give way to juicy blue berries about the size of blueberries or somewhat smaller.

Range and Habitat

Creeping Oregon grape is found from British Columbia to Colorado and Texas and throughout the West to California; spottily in the northeastern United States. Tall Oregon grape is more a plant of the Northwest and is found from British Columbia and Alberta to Idaho, Oregon, and California; sparsely throughout the northeastern United States. Grows in forests, forest edges, dappled shade, and sometimes full sun. Found in low to mid elevations.

Comments

These little berries range from sour to delicious. They can be eaten raw, cooked, or dried. I have heard that in the wet climate of the Northwest they are much sweeter than in the dry climate of the Four Corners region. I have found delicious berries from the creeping mahonia in Colorado, even in summers of drought. If you find a sweet juicy one, you'll be very happy. This is also a common garden plant and usually considered purely ornamental. Not so.

Berries can be made into a beverage like grape juice or made into jam. The stem, root, and leaves are used for medicinal purposes.

RECIPE

Mahonia Juice

Collect 1 cup berries and place in blender. Add water just to cover berries; blend well. Strain through a colander, collecting the juice in a bowl below. Place juice back into blender with 6 ice cubes and 2 cups watermelon. Add honey if desired. Blend until combined.

Serve in chilled glass with a pinch of cinnamon on top or with a whole cinnamon stick for stirring.

COMMON JUNIPER
Juniperus communis

Family: Cupressaceae

Other names: Common juniper, dwarf juniper, prostrate juniper, mountain juniper, old field common juniper, ground juniper

Description

Native spreading evergreen shrub or small tree. In the Rockies, common juniper is most often seen as an undulating, mat-forming ground cover or shrub that can reach about 4'9" in height (often shorter) and 13' wide. Needle-like leaves are stubby and green.

The small cones (less than ½") look like round seeds or berries and can be easily recognized as juniper "berries." Young berries are green and tender, turning dark blue, purplish or blue-black with maturity at around eighteen months.

Range and Habitat

The USDA Forest Service says this might possibly be the most widely distributed tree in the world. From Alaska and northern Canada to New Mexico and around the globe.

FORAGER NOTE: Leaves are like needles, not cedar-like (i.e., not scaled). Obvious berries, usually year-round.

Comments

Food for deer, mountain goats, and other species, especially in winter and early spring. A popular home landscaping staple.

This long-cultivated variety is extremely popular in home landscapes. It grows vigorously and often gets out of control, taking up too much room in the limited space given. Most people have seen this or related varieties in home gardens across the United States but ignored its edible and medicinal qualities. As long as you do not use poisons on your lawn or garden, common juniper can make a great start to your year-round backyard pantry.

Usually eat one to three berries. Let your tongue tell you when you have had enough.

RECIPE

Holiday Necklaces

Pick a bowl full of juniper berries. Using a strong needle and thread, carefully press needle through berries and make a necklace as long as you like. It's easiest to make it long enough to fit over your head and just tie the ends of the thread together. Use berries of varying color, from light green to dark purple, for an interesting pattern. Add some rose hips for variation.

RECIPE

Lemonade Cocktail with Fresh Juniper

Soak a handful of juniper berries in a bottle of gin or vodka for several weeks. The alcohol will take on the strong juniper flavor, depending on how many you use. Juniper berries are traditionally used to make gin, and an extra "fresh-hopped" addition of the berries makes an exciting and earthy treat. Mix and serve on ice with sparkling lemonade or other light mixer that allows you to taste the juniper.

Variation: Make a juniper mojito by combing fresh-crushed mint, a bit of sugar or other sweetener, and juniper-infused vodka with fresh-squeezed lime juice and ice. Shake well.

ROCKY MOUNTAIN JUNIPER
Juniperus scopulorum

Family: Cupressaceae

Other names: Rocky Mountain cedar, mountain red cedar

WARNING: Some accounts warn that this plant can cause kidney failure, convulsions, and irritated digestive tract with overdoses. Pregnant women, children under age 12, people with cancer, and people with kidney disease should **not** ingest.

Description

This native perennial evergreen is an erect shrub that often appears more like a small tree. It forms a dense conical or pyramidal shape that grows from 3'–33' tall and when mature is usually about 20'–30' tall. Leaves begin as needle-like and when mature are covered in small scales earning it the name, cedar-like juniper.

Rocky Mountain juniper also has a prolific array of small, hard, powdery blue or purplish ovulate cones about ¼"–⅜" in diameter that most people refer

> FORAGER NOTE: Cedar-like scaled leaves or needles. Obvious berries, usually year-round.

to as berries. Seeds mature in their second year. Green in the first year, they turn deep blue or purple.

Trees live for 250 to 300 years, some for 1,000 years. They begin producing seeds at 10 to 20 years but are most productive from about 50 to 200 years.

Rocky Mountain juniper reproduces by seeds and is pollinated mostly by wind. Hybridizes with other species, which may cause some difficulty in identification.

Range and Habitat
Rocky Mountain juniper is found on dry, rocky slopes from British Columbia and Alberta to Texas. Can be used for screens or hedges. Hardy to USDA Zone 3. Requires only 10" of rain per year. Found near sea level in the Northwest and up to 9,000' in the Southwest. Climax species in juniper and piñon-juniper habitats. Common species that is important for both humans and wildlife throughout the region.

Comments
Light green, blue, or purple berries are edible. Berries are strong tasting, sort of like peppercorns but not really. Younger, green berries are more astringent. Older, blue berries are sweeter. I nibble on both while on the trail. This is not the kind of berry, like blueberries, you would eat a big bowl of. It's more of a

Raw Juniper Berries

One of the most rewarding ways to eat wild foods is raw, straight from the plant. It allows you to experience the plant and understand its properties in a pure and powerful form that just doesn't happen when it gets mixed up in a fancy recipe.

Hiking along any trail in our region, you will pass one form of juniper or another. I like to pick the green tender berries and the older blue ones. See warning above, and don't overconsume.

Variation: Eat 1 juniper berry together with 1 rose hip. (Seeds are edible.) Both can be found hanging from bushes year-round.

flavoring or spice to be used in small quantities, about one to three berries at a time. It can also be chewed like a mint to freshen breath.

Juniper is well known as the flavoring ingredient in gin. The berries are extremely flavorful, and a small amount goes a long way. Can be harvested year-round at any time during the berry's life cycle. Can be used as a spice like pepper or rosemary, cooked with meats or fish, or used as medicinal tea. When cooking with meat, a good rule of thumb is to use six berries per pound of meat. Use fresh or dried.

Rocky Mountain juniper provides dense, protective shelter for wildlife and migratory birds, including chipping sparrows, robins, song sparrows, mockingbirds, sharp-shinned hawks, juncos, and myrtle warblers; also mice, voles, and wood rats. Large game animals also utilize Rocky Mountain juniper for forage and protection.

RECIPE

Simple Lamb or Venison Stew with Crushed Juniper Berries

Combine in a slow cooker: 2 pounds lamb or venison with bones, 12 crushed fresh or dried juniper berries, 4 carrots (chopped), 4 stalks celery (chopped), 3 potatoes (cubed), ½ cup black-eyed peas, ½ teaspoon turmeric, 5 bay leaves, 1 jalapeño (or less to taste). Fill slow cooker with water.

Cook on high for several hours. Once beans are soft and fully cooked, add salt and pepper to taste. Add additional water during cooking if needed.

CANADA BUFFALOBERRY
Shepherdia canadensis

Family: Elaeagnaceae
Other names: Soapberry, buffalo-berry, russet buffaloberry, russet red buffaloberry, Canadian buffalo-berry, *Hippophae canadensis, Elaeagnus canadensis, Lepargyrea canadensis*
WARNING: Fruits contain saponin, which can be harmful if eaten in large quantities.

> ### RECIPE
>
> **Indian Ice Cream**
>
> In a clean (not greasy and not plastic) bowl, combine 2 cups buffaloberries and 2 cups water. Beat mixture well by hand or with a metal mixer until it becomes foamy, like a soft meringue. Add honey or other sweetener, and beat in. Serve as a bitter-sweet desert.
>
> **NOTE:** Contact with grease or plastic will prevent froth from forming.

Description

Native perennial, nitrogen-fixing shrub grows from 3'–13' tall. Oval leaves are dark green and opposite, ¾"–2⅓" long. The distinguishing characteristics are the small but prominent rust-colored spots on the under surface of the leaves, along with silvery hairs. Flowers are yellow to brownish. Fruits are red or yellowish berrylike achenes. Fruits ripen from midsummer to early fall. May be stunted (as in the photo) in drought years.

Range and Habitat

From Alaska and northern Canada across the western United States to New Mexico and California and across to the Northeast. Grows in sun or dappled shade.

Comments

Fruit has high saponin content and can therefore be used as soap. Fruit can also be eaten raw, dried, or cooked. Berries are sweeter after the first frost. There are also a variety of medicinal uses.

KINNIKINNICK
Arctostaphylos uva ursi

Family: Ericaceae
Other names: Bearberry, Indian tobacco, hog cranberry, *uva ursi*, beargrape, creeping man-zanita, coralillo, kinnik-kinnik, k'nickk'neck
Lookalikes: Cranberry, lingonberry, mountain cranberry, creeping snowberry
WARNING: Some sources warn that *uva ursi* should not be used by pregnant women. It is reported to cause decreased blood flow to the fetus. I have not confirmed whether this applies to smoking the leaves, eating the berries, or some other use.

Description
This perennial subshrub blankets forest floors throughout the region. Dark green leaves are small, rounded, spoon or heart shaped with a distinct cleft or vein running their length. Leaves are sturdy, evergreen, and leathery or plastic feeling. The shrub reaches a height of 8"–10", though often less.

> FORAGER NOTE: In late summer and fall, look for bright red berries in the forest ground cover.

Small pink or cream flowers give way to very mealy bright red berries. The berries can be confused with cranberries and lingonberries but are much mealier. Bearberries also have several larger seeds inside, which cranberries and lingonberries lack.

Range and Habitat

From Alaska and the Northwest Territories south across western North America through New Mexico. From 3,000'–9,000' in elevation, but beginning higher in the southern reaches of the range.

Comments

Dried leaves are a traditional smoking herb. People commonly refer to *uva ursi* as kinnikinnick, although the Native American word *kinnikinnick* is said to refer to a smoking mixture usually containing a variety of bark and leaves that often included *uva ursi*.

The plant is also called bearberry because bears are thought to be fond of eating the berries. Leaves can be used to tan hides. Like cranberries, good for urinary tract health.

RECIPE

Pemmican

Think about what it would take to really survive off the land without the grocery store or the freezer. You would use what was available and figure out ways to make it last through winter. Pemmican is just that—a mixture of rendered fat (suet), dried meat, dried fruits or berries, nuts, and seeds.

Blend well in a blender or food processor, 2 cups dried meat; place in a bowl. In blender chop 1½ cups dried *uva ursi* berries and ¼ cup raw pine nuts or sunflower seeds. Add to bowl. Mix in 1 cup warm (just liquid) suet. Massage together well with hands or a wooden spoon. Spread out in thin layer onto a cookie sheet, and allow to cool. Slice into strips and store in a sealed container. Great trail snack throughout the year.

Variation: Add honey to mixture.

CURRANTS
Ribes spp.

Family: Grossulariaceae

Lookalikes: Thimbleberry and Boulder raspberry (larger leaves of similar shapes), Rocky Mountain maple (no berries), prickly currants (very similar but with lots of thorns), gooseberries

Related species: Northern black currant (*R. hudsonianum*), wax currant (*R. cereum*), golden currant (*R. aureum*)

WARNING: Some reports say that large quantities can cause nausea and even vomiting. Normal quantities of consumption are fine for most people.

FORAGER NOTE: The dried flower withers and hangs from the berry. This is perfectly fine to eat, but many prefer to remove it, especially when eating currants raw. Although the flower pulls off easily, it is small and time-consuming to remove.

Description
Currants are a native, deciduous smooth-barked shrub ranging 1'–6' tall. Branches are erect and arching.

Small tubular white, pinkish, or greenish elongated, five-sepaled clusters of two to eight flowers give way to clusters of mild-flavored berries in late summer or fall. In drought years the process can speed up and berries can be seen by midsummer.

Currant leaves can take on two distinct forms. Some are fan-shaped and rounded, with shallow, rounded lobes (wax currant). Others are more deeply, sharply lobed like a maple leaf (golden currant). Leaves are alternate or in clusters.

Berries and leaves have resin glands that can make the berries appear dusty. Currant fruits are bright red, red-orange, golden-yellow, or black and often appear somewhat translucent.

The golden currant (*R. aureum*) is named for its golden flowers. The fruit is a smooth berry that is green when immature. It ripens from yellow to red to black or dark purple.

Range and Habitat
Dry sunny hillsides, forest edges, ridges, sagebrush fields, and disturbed areas from British Columbia to northern Texas. Hardy bushes are prolific; they literally grow out of rocks. They can be found thriving in dry and rocky soil throughout the region from about 5,000'–13,000' in elevation. Bushes grow larger with moisture.

Comments
Berries and young leaves are edible. Berries can be eaten raw or cooked. My favorite way to eat currants is after riding my bicycle along a rural mountain road and finding this sweet wild snack, or after climbing to the top of a rock cliff and coming upon a precariously perched currant shrub growing out of the rock.

One fall afternoon while taking a roadside break with our bicycles, my husband and I found ourselves standing on a high ridge in the foothills outside of Boulder, Colorado. We were surrounded by a rolling field dotted with 4'-high currant bushes, all filled with bright reddish-orange berries. The aspen trees were turning yellow, and we could see for miles in all directions and up to the

Continental Divide, where snow had recently dusted the high peaks. I smelled a whiff of sage and realized that fall was settling into the Rocky Mountains. This is currant season. As I slowly picked wild currants from the great expanse, I thought about how many of these delicate little berries the local bears must pick to nourish their massive bodies in preparation for their winter slumber. This is slow-going work, but I get a sense that it has been done before, right here in this very field, and not just by human hands.

RECIPE

Hearty Wild Currant Pancakes

Place your favorite organic multigrain pancake mix in a bowl. (The type that only needs water is best if you are out camping.) Add a pinch of fresh-ground nutmeg and ⅛ teaspoon fresh-ground cinnamon. Add water as directed. Stir gently.

Heat skillet to medium-high. Add generous amounts of butter, coconut oil, or bacon grease and heat. Spoon pancake batter onto skillet, and immediately add 1 teaspoon currants to each pancake. Flip when air bubbles begin to pop. Serve with real maple syrup or unbleached fair trade sugar.

Variation: Add chopped almonds and flax seeds.

RECIPE

Lemon Pudding with Fresh Wild Currants

Begin to heat water in double boiler. Also heat 2 cups of water in a separate pot to a boil. While water is heating, sift together 3 tablespoons cornstarch, 1 tablespoon flour, 1¾ cups granulated sugar. Whisk in the 2 cups boiling water until mixture becomes smooth. When water in bottom level of double boiler is simmering, add the flour-water mixture to the top dry pot; cook for 5 minutes, stirring occasionally.

In a separate bowl beat 4 egg yolks. Stir several tablespoons of the hot mixture into the beaten egg yolks (to temper), then slowly add the beaten egg yolks to the hot mixture; continue simmering in the double boiler. Stir in grated rind of 2 lemons, 1 tablespoon butter, ¼ teaspoon salt, and ¼ cup lemon juice. Stirring constantly, cook until the mixture becomes smooth and thick.

Spoon into bowls, and top with fresh currants. Serve at any temperature.

Variation: Add a dollop of meringue or whipped cream.

PRICKLY CURRANT
Ribes lacustre

Family: Grossulariaceae
Other names: Bristly black currant
Related species: Mountain prickly currant (*R. montigenum*)
WARNING: Getting pricked by the spines can cause allergic reactions in some people.

Description
Very similar to nonprickly currant species. This native shrub is rambling and leggy, from 1½'–5' tall and covered in obvious sharp spines, or thorns. Flowers are pink or coral.

Berries of *R. lacustre* are black. Bristly black currant is a native perennial that grows to about 3'–4' in height. Berries of *R. montigenum* are red.

Range and Habitat
R. lacustre has a larger geographic range than *R. montigenum*. It is found from Alaska east throughout Canada and south through Colorado and California.

Found in shrublands, clear-cut areas, the subalpine zone, woods, and riparian woodlands.

R. montigenum is found throughout the western half of the United States and British Columbia. Found in alpine and subalpine zones.

Comments

Berries are eaten by bears, birds, and rodents.

> RECIPE
>
> Use in the same ways you would use regular currants.

WILD PLUMS
Prunus americana

Family: Rosaceae
Other names: American plum, goose plum, river plum

Description

This native perennial shrub or small tree grows from 3'–33' tall. In the Rockies it more frequently looks like a brambly shrub. Leaves are typical of the stone fruits—ovate, usually with pointed tips, sharp teeth, and reaching 3"–5" long. Can form thickets by underground-spreading root systems. Although individual shrubs are short-lived (twenty years or so), the stand can live far longer.

Inflorescences are single or in clusters of two to four fragrant, showy white flowers, about 1" each. Fruits are somewhat smaller than commercial plum varieties but still quite plump and fleshy. They are yellowish, bright rose, reddish, purplish, or orange-ish drupes or stone fruits. The seed is a typical pit (although smaller), as in commercial plum varieties. Ripens in late summer to early fall.

Range and Habitat

From Saskatchewan and Manitoba to New Mexico and Arizona and across portions of the eastern United States. Requires at least 16" of rainfall per year so in the arid West is usually found along streambanks, ditches, or other moist riparian habitats or in meadows with moisture-capturing depressions. Often found

in canyons mixed in with grapevines and chokecherries and along roadsides. Up to about 7,500' elevation in New Mexico (somewhat lower farther north).

Comments

I literally get goose bumps when I think about wild plums. They're that good. Eat them raw, dried, stewed, as jam, in pie, grilled, as fruit leather, with muesli, or whatever you can come up with. Beware: There are so many wild plums growing along roadside ditches throughout our region, being on the lookout will seriously impair your Fall driving safety.

RECIPE

Grilled Plum and Goat Cheese Salad

Slice plums in half and remove pit. Prepare salad with mixed greens from the garden (baby kale, chard, dandelion greens, lamb's-quarter, and a few amaranth leaves). Combine organic olive oil with good balsamic vinegar and a touch of honey. Mix well, and toss with salad greens.

Grill halved plums over low to medium heat, turning to prevent sticking and burning.

Serve in individual bowls with several grilled plums per person. Top with crumbled goat cheese and fresh-ground green pepper.

RECIPE

Dried Wild Plums

Harvest a basketful of plums. Remove seeds if desired, but it's not at all necessary. Place on racks of food dehydrator. Dry until plums are dried but not hard as rock. Some moisture is OK.

Store in a sealed jar through winter. Enjoy as a snack on their own or in baked goods or winter stews or compotes.

CHOKECHERRY
Prunus virginiana

Family: Rosaceae

Other names: Chokecherries, wild black cherry, *Padus virginiana*

Lookalikes: Common buckthorn/European buckthorn (not edible), serviceberry (edible)

WARNING: Hydrocyanic acid causes the seed, bark, and leaves to be toxic. Seeds (which are like small plum pits) are poisonous. **Do not** eat them.

Description

This native perennial is a deciduous thicket-forming shrub or small tree growing 6'–40' high. Sometimes takes the shape of a tree but often grows as thickets with thin trunks about 6" wide. It has extensive rhizomatic root systems and reproduces either by spreading rhizomes or by seed.

Chokecherry leaves are shiny, alternate, oval or oblong, with tiny jaggedly toothed edges. They are green, with the underside lighter than the top, turning yellow in fall. Similar to the leaves of other stone fruits, chokecherry leaves are 1"–4" long; the width is about half the length.

Small, nicely scented flowers are white and form together in showy, tubular drooping

clusters or racemes 3"–6" long. Flowers in spring to summer.

Fruits are available from late summer to early fall. Fruits are tart, dark drupes about ¼" in diameter. The berrylike fruits hang in elongated clusters mimicking the shape of the flower clusters.

Range and Habitat

From Alaska south across most of the United States. Absent from several of the southeastern states. Found commonly in the foothills and canyons of the Rocky Mountains, especially next to creeks and ditches.

Comments

Chokecherries are very common. The plant is named for its astringent mouth-puckering quality; however, the edibility of raw chokecherries varies by plant and location. While I find some cherries are not enjoyable to eat raw, most are delicious right off the branch. Chokecherry is commonly used to make jam, syrup, and wine. It goes well on a big slice of fresh toast or homemade pancakes.

Note that the seeds are very hard and would break a juicer. You are warned. A Foley food mill works much better for removing pits from flesh.

Despite the warning that the seeds are poisonous, it is fine to boil them with the fruits before separating them out. This does not seem to cause any problems. Also, you can eat chokecherries raw and then spit out the seeds. Having them in your mouth as you remove the soft flesh with your teeth is perfectly safe. They are very hard, and there is no real danger of breaking through the pit with your teeth.

RECIPE

Chokecherry Jelly

Wash cherries and remove stems. Simmer 4 cups chokecherries in enough water to cover the fruit. While simmering, mash the fruit with a wooden spoon. Remove from heat and run cherries though a Foley mill, retaining the liquid and pulp in a bowl below.

Put juice-pulp mixture back into a saucepan. Combine with 1 packet pectin. Bring to a boil and then add 1–2 cups sugar or other sweetener. Stir well. Bring to a rolling boil; continue boiling for 1 minute, stirring constantly. Remove from heat and place in jars. Store in refrigerator.

NOTE: For long-term storage use canning methods appropriate for jelly. Place in sterilized glass jars with sealed lids, as you would other jellies. **Variation:** Use half fresh apple cider and half chokecherry juice.

WILD ROSES
Rosa spp.

Family: Rosaceae

Related species: Common species include Woods' rose (*R. woodsii*), prickly rose (*R. acicularis*), and Nootka rose (*R. nutkana*).

WARNING: Some accounts warn to not eat the seeds because they contain cyanide compounds and have hairs that cause discomfort.

Description

This lovely native perennial shrub is spreading, can form dense thickets, and grows 1'–10' high (often around 3'–4'). Stems are thorny. Leaves are alternate, and each leaf consists of five to nine leaflets (pinnately divided) that look the same as cultivated rose leaves. Leaves have one oblong, serrate leaflet at the tip of the leaf stem, with one to four pairs of matching, opposite leaflets. Leaflets are ½"–2" long.

Beautifully rose-scented, five-petaled light to dark pink flowers are 2"–4" wide and flower in spring to summer. The round central disc of pollinating parts is yellow.

About fifteen to thirty-five seeds are encased in a fruit called a rose hip. Rose hips look somewhat like red currants but thicker, meatier, and not as translucent.

Like currants, the shriveled flower is often still hanging from the fruit. Rose hips can vary significantly in size and color, from big, shiny, and bright red to smaller, duller, or more subtly colored. They are about ¼"– ½" long.

Range and Habitat

From Alaska to California and Texas. Considering the high price of commercial roses, you'd think wild roses would be rare, but they are not. Wild roses are found almost everywhere around our region. I see them prolifically along roadsides, streambanks, and trails from the plains to mid-elevations. They grow larger with moisture and loose soil but also grow in dry and more-compacted areas.

RECIPE

Fried Tofu with Sweet-Spicy Rose Hip Sauce

It seems like the hot peppers in my garden are ready at just about the same time as the rose hips, so why not try them out together. To make the sauce, combine ½ cup rose hips (fresh or dry) with 3 cups water; simmer for about 10 minutes. Remove from heat, and smash the rose hips so the seeds pop out. Simmer for 10 minutes more; remove from heat.

Strain liquid to remove the seeds. Return liquid to saucepan. Add a few hot peppers, diced. The amount varies depending on how spicy the pepper is and how spicy you want the sauce to be. Add 1 heaping tablespoon sugar or honey; simmer all for 10 minutes, stirring frequently.

Mix ½ teaspoon organic cornstarch with a little bit of water. Add to simmering mixture, and stir in well. Sauce will thicken. Cover and turn off heat.

Variation: Add a dash of soy sauce, fish sauce, and some ginger while simmering.

Slice extra-firm tofu into large slices about ½" thick. Heat skillet with ⅛" to ¼" olive or canola oil to medium-high. Flick a drip of water on the hot oil. The oil is ready if it sputters on contact. Fry tofu on each side until browned and firm. Remove from heat.

Serve tofu on a bed of chopped lettuce, and pour plenty of rose hip sauce over tofu. Sprinkle some chopped green onions on top.

Comments

Rose hips (fruits) and flowers can be eaten raw, cooked, or dried. Flowers make a nice garnish for sweets and salads. Rose hips are used as a base for rose hip jam (*champe*). Fruits can also be used to make necklaces and garlands. Rose hips can be made into sauces both spicy and sweet. Rose hips can be eaten at any stage and are especially good after a frost sets the sugars.

Over one hundred species in the *Rosa* genus and many cultivars. Several wild rose species are found in the Rockies; they hybridize with one another, so exact species identification can be difficult. Luckily it is not necessary, as all rose species can be used interchangeably.

Despite the warning above, I know many people who eat rose hip seeds. Best to eat in moderation. As with all new foods, increase amounts slowly to see how you react, and keep it part of a diverse, well-rounded diet. Personally, I love eating rose hips at all stages of development (fresh to dried) while out on the trail.

RASPBERRY
Rubus spp.

Family: Rosaceae
Other names: Wild red raspberry, American red raspberry. *Rubus idaeus* is the most common species in the Rocky Mountain region.
Lookalikes: Thimbleberry, black raspberry (*R. leucodermis*)

Description
Low-growing deciduous shrub with a perennial root system that sends up biennial stalks from which small five-petaled flowers produce red raspberries in late summer or fall. The shrubs grow 1'–10' high but are usually seen throughout the Rockies closer to 3'–4' in height. Sharply pointed leaves are alternate and pinnately compound in leaflets of three to five.

Like its relative the rose, raspberry is also covered in thorns, so take care when picking. Fruits are actually aggregates of drupelets that are commonly referred to as berries. Berry size and production can vary widely depending on the plant and conditions. Wild raspberries are generally smaller than commercial varieties.

Old Fashioned Raspberry Pie

This is my Grandma Buddy's old-fashioned pie recipe, with a few variations. I learned it with a Crisco crust, but here is a slightly healthier variation.

Preheat oven to 405°F.

Filling:
Measure proper amount of raspberries by filling your empty pie dish to overflowing. Transfer berries to large bowl. Add ¾ cup unbleached cane sugar, grated rind of ¼ lemon, and 4 tablespoons tapioca pearls. Stir gently to combine; set aside.

Crust:
Using a food processor with the metal blade, pulse to combine ingredients.

Prepare chilled water by filling a bowl with water and placing a few ice cubes in the bowl. Set aside.

Combine 2 cups white pastry flour and 1 teaspoon salt. Cut in ¼ cup coconut oil, and ½ cup organic canola oil until mixture resembles coarse crumbs with some small pea-size pieces. Sprinkle in 2–4 tablespoons chilled water, 1 tablespoon at a time, and pulse to combine. If needed add 2–4 additional tablespoons of the chilled water and combine. Dough should be workable, not too wet and not too dry. Don't overmix.

Shape dough into two even balls. Roll out one ball at a time, one for the top crust and one for the bottom crust. Roll dough on a lightly floured work surface into circles 2" wider than the pie plate. Transfer one section to pie plate, and gently press along the bottom.

Fill unbaked pie crust with the raspberry mixture. Add a few slices of butter to the top of the heap if desired. Place the top crust on top of the berries; fold and pinch edges to secure top crust to bottom crust. Using a fork, poke a few holes in the top crust. Place pie in preheated 405°F oven. After 10 minutes, reduce heat to 350°F and bake for about 45 minutes to 1 hour, or until juice is actively bubbling out of the crust and the crust is just beginning to brown.

NOTE: Place a cookie sheet under the pie plate to catch any juice overflow.

Range and Habitat

Raspberries are generally widespread throughout the United States. *R. idaeus* is also widespread but is not found in the southern states from Texas to Florida. Found in disturbed areas, sun-dappled openings in forests, and along roadways and woodland borders. Also found on steep slopes but usually smaller here. Does well in full sun and partial shade. Can tolerate both dry and moist conditions. Hardy to USDA Zone 3.

Comments

Raspberries are primarily pollinated by bees.

Berries, leaves, and roots are edible. Berries can be eaten raw or cooked. Leaves can be used fresh or dried as tea. Leaves are said to be useful for the female reproductive tract, uterine health, and alleviating menstrual cramps.

Leaves should be harvested when the leaf is still green. Make tea with fresh leaves or fully dry leaves. Some accounts say that partially dried leaves are not good for this use.

The psychological aspect of foraging cannot be overstated. Most people in our culture have no experience with picking and eating wild plants and have a huge mental barrier to doing so. Part of the hesitance is the fear of eating something poisonous. This is of course totally rational. Overcoming this fear is not just a mental exercise. It takes serious study of wild plants. Some species require more study than others. Raspberries are a great gateway wild edible because most of us already know what they look like and have spent our lives eating them. Learning to identify them in the wild is easier for this reason.

With proper precauction, raspberries can't reasonably be mistaken for anything poisonous, and they are incredibly prevalent throughout the Rocky Mountain region. They grow along trails (sunny disturbed areas especially) throughout the entire United States, so the beginner has access to wild raspberries even on easy hiking trails.

RECIPE

Hot Cereal and Fresh Raspberries

An excellent addition to oatmeal or cream of wheat. Great while camping. Prepare hot cereal according to instructions for that cereal. Add a few fresh-picked wild raspberries. Top with a spoonful of crushed almonds or walnuts and local honey.

THIMBLEBERRY
Rubus parviflorus

Family: Rosaceae

Other names: Western thimbleberry, salmonberry, white-flowering raspberry, western thimble raspberry

Related species: Boulder raspberry (*Oreobatus deliciosus*), delicious raspberry (*Rubus deliciosus*)

Lookalikes: Baneberries (poisonous), raspberries (berries), currants (leaves), Rocky Mountain maple (leaves)

WARNINGS: The leaves of thimbleberry look very similar to those of the poisonous baneberry. The berries are totally different.

Description

This little-known native perennial shrub has some of the best-tasting wild berries in the Rockies. It has large leaves and is thornless. Fairly large white flowers (rarely pink) have five distinct white petals with obvious fuzzy yellow stamens forming a big round yellow center. Flowers are up to 2½" across.

Thimbleberry (*R. parviflorus*) has flowers in clusters of two to seven. Its leaves are about 4"–8" wide. Boulder raspberry (*Oreobatus deliciosus*) has solitary flowers. Its leaves are smaller, about 1"–2" wide.

Thimbleberry leaves are palmate, like a maple leaf, somewhat fuzzy and soft, with five shallow lobes. The largest leaves are about the size of a hand with outstretched fingers. The lobes can be pointed. Boulder raspberry leaves are more rounded and not fuzzy, somewhat waxy looking in comparison. They look similar to the leaves of the wax currant but larger.

Thimbleberry grows from 1'–8' tall. Each spindly, scraggly cane lives two to three years. First year primocanes do not produce fruit. After that they may become branched and productive, sometimes reaching 8' tall. Greenish twigs have fine hairs. Reseeds in disturbed areas and can form dense thickets via its underground rhizomes.

Numerous drupelets form a berrylike cluster. "Berries" are like large raspberries but bigger and softer. Found alone (boulder raspberry) or in groups of two to seven (thimbleberry).

Range and Habitat

Alaska and British Columbia, across the western United States to New Mexico. Grows in woods, on open hillsides, in avalanche chutes, and along streambanks. Found in both moist and dry areas. From 3,500'–9,500' elevation.

Comments

Berries and young shoots are edible. Many accounts say that thimbleberries are dry and tasteless. When I finally found and tasted my first thimbleberry, I immediately thought I had eaten the wrong plant because it was so incredible soft, juicy, and sweet. Young shoots can be eaten, and leaves are used for medicinal purposes. Can be cultivated by transplanting rhizomes.

The best way to eat these is raw, straight from the branch. Take care picking, as they are quite mushy. If saving for later, use a study container (not a bag) to harvest and transport the berries.

RECIPE

Thimbleberry Tofu Pudding

Harvest ¼ cup thimbleberries. Cut 1 block firm tofu into quarters; place in a blender. Add 3 tablespoons brown sugar and a dash of vanilla. Add ⅛ teaspoon cinnamon. Add 3 tablespoons water (more or less depending on how much liquid your blender needs to work correctly). Blend until very smooth and creamy. Add the thimbleberries and blend in briefly.

Pour pudding into a bowl, using a soft spatula to scrape the sides of the blender. Serve immediately at room temperature, or chill in refrigerator for 2 hours or more and serve cold. Save a few berries to put on top as garnish.

Trees

TREES: DECIDUOUS

RUSSIAN OLIVE
Elaeagnus angustifolia

Family: Elaeagnaceae
Other names: Russian silverberry, oleaster

Description

This Eurasian native is a deciduous shrub or small tree that grows 12'–45' tall. It is a somewhat gangly, bushy, smallish tree with distinct powdery, silver-green oblong or linear leaves that are long and thin and sometimes curl into a partial tube shape. Its fruits grow in drupes and are like small gray-green olives, although not related to commercial varieties of olives. They ripen in late summer or early fall.

The roots are nitrogen fixers, allowing Russian olive to thrive even in very poor soil.

Range and Habitat

Russian olive is a massively invasive nonnative and is now very common along ditches, creeks, and rivers throughout the region from about 4,500'–6,000' in elevation.

Comments

The fruits can be eaten raw, dried, cooked, or made into a beverage. Fruits are astringent and are best when fully ripened. They are also mealy (less mealy than *uva ursi* berries though). Can be used as a seasoning or to make sorbet or jelly. High in vitamins A, C, and E and also in essential fatty acids and flavonoids. They can be blended with water to make a beverage that is mildly sweet. Best to strain out or eat around the seeds.

The sale of Russian olive trees is banned in Colorado, and they are considered an extreme nuisance species, so harvest fruits freely. They like riverbanks and riparian areas, use a lot of water, and are accused of crowding out native species like cottonwood (although river diversions and dams have also played a significant role in the cottonwood's decline). Russian olives now provide shelter and food for birds like pheasants and others.

Not related to the culinary species of olives. The fruits look similar but are smaller than most commercial olives.

RECIPE

Russian Olive Jelly

Wash fruits and remove stems. Simmer 4 cups Russian olive fruits in enough water to cover them. Simmer for about 30 minutes, mashing the fruit with a wooden spoon. Remove from heat and run though a Foley mill, retaining the liquid and pulp in a bowl below.

Put juice-pulp mixture back into a saucepan. Combine with 1 packet of pectin. Bring to a boil, and then add ½ cup sugar or other sweetener if desired. Stir well. Bring to a rolling boil and stir constantly for 1 minute while boiling. Remove from heat and place in jars; store in refrigerator.

For long-term storage, use canning methods appropriate for jelly. Place in sterilized glass jars with sealed lids, as you would other jellies.

Variation: For a savory jelly, instead of sugar, use fresh or dried hot peppers and a little bit of salt.

GAMBEL OAK
Quercus gambelii

Family: Fagaceae
Other names: Scrub oak, Rocky Mountain white oak, Utah white oak
WARNING: Contains tannic acid, which can be poisonous if great quantities are consumed. Cattle will become ill if more than 50 percent of their diet is from oak. Frost increases toxicity.

Description

Common, native shrub oak with green, deeply lobed, waxy, alternate leaves. Seven to eleven rounded lobes per leaf, but exact leaf shape is variable. Scraggly shrub or small tree up to 75' high but often significantly shorter, more like 10'– 35' tall. Moisture availability has an impact on height. Foliage does not often turn red like that of its eastern relatives.

Male catkins produce pollen and pollinate the female flowers, which each produce one acorn. Acorns are about ¾" long and are held by a cap about one-third the size of the nut. Other acorn species have different-size caps; some even totally encapsulate the seed (acorn).

Complex root system consist of lignotubers (bud-producing swellings at the base of the stalk). They also have deep-feeding roots and rhizomes and sprout clones to form thickets of shrub oak. Also reproduces by seed, but vegetative spreading is more successful.

Range and Habitat

Wyoming and Nevada to Colorado and New Mexico and sparsely in Texas; also South Dakota. Dry slopes and canyons in the foothills and high deserts from about 3,300'–9,900' in elevation.

Comments

Acorns can be eaten raw, boiled, or roasted. Also can be dried and ground into flour. Gambel acorns can be eaten raw, though many would argue that point. If the acorns you want to eat have an unpleasant taste, it is because they are high in tannins. In that case you should leach them. Acorns are usually soaked in water or boiled to leach out the tannins and bitterness. If they taste good raw, they are safe to eat without leaching.

Bark is used for medicinal teas. Raw nuts can be stored in the freezer. Very important for a wide range of wildlife, including deer, elk, bighorn sheep, squirrels, owls and other birds.

To prepare acorns, first remove the shells and testa (papery skin). For cold leaching, grind acorns in a food processor, food mill, or blender or by smashing them with a stone into a powder. For cold leaching, soak powder in several changes of water (a few days to a week). Then, lay it out in trays and dry in the

---

RECIPE

Homemade Acorn Milk

Blend ½ cup acorns and ½ cup raw almonds in a blender filled with water. Blend very well. Strain milk though a fine colander. Use as milk with granola cereal or muesli. Retain the mush and use for recipe below or for granola or cookies. Retain pulp for Dehydrator Acorn Crackers, homemade granola, or cookies.

Variation: Add honey or maple syrup to sweeten the acorn milk.

NOTE: If your acorns are high in tannin and bitter to the taste, leach first.

Dehydrator Acorn Crackers

Cold-leach if desired, or use pulp from Homemade Acorn Milk. Use freshly leached acorn flour (not dried).

Start with 2 cups acorn mush. Add ¼ cup chopped fresh chives. (My chives are usually giving me a second harvest about when the acorns are ready, so this is a good combination, but other herbs are great too.) Add salt, pepper, tamari, and hot chili to taste. Put herbs in blender or food processor, and blend well with acorn mush. Spread out onto a lightly oiled cookie sheet and bake at very low heat until crisp but not fully browned. Preferably, use a food dehydrator.

Variation: Substitute fresh or roasted poblano chiles for the chives.

sun, in an oven on the lowest setting, or in a food dehydrator. For cold leaching, crushed acorns can also be subjected to constant running water.

For hot leaching, acorns do not have be ground into a flour but can be crushed in half or into quarters. For hot leaching (which removes nutrients and good fats) boil until no longer bitter.

Alkali solutions of lye and lime can also be used to help neutralize the tannins. These products work well but can be toxic if not handled properly. There are countless ways to leach acorns, so it is advisable to read multiple accounts to determine what method will work best for you.

APPLE
Malus domestica

Family: Rosaceae

Other names: Orchard apple, table apple

WARNING: Apple seeds contain hydrogen cyanide and are toxic if eaten in large quantities. Too much causes respiratory failure, even death.

Description

As one of the world's most-beloved fruits, there are more than 7,500 cultivated varieties of this species. Native to western Asia, where it was first cultivated thousands of years ago.

Small trees, sometimes rambling looking, with many branches and full leaves. Apple trees are somewhat squat and grow 14'–33' tall.

Simple, alternate leaves are serrated and 1"–4" long. Clusters of white, pink, or red five-petaled flowers. Apples vary in size and can be from red to green. Apples also vary in taste from sour to sweet, depending on the variety.

Dried Apples

I love this simple recipe. Having unadulterated, perfectly dried apples in the pantry through winter is a huge (and cheap and healthy) treat. This is great even with the sourest apples.

Leaving a square around the core, slice apples into quarters. If large, slice each quarter in half. Place in bowl with fresh-squeezed lime juice, and toss. After slicing a few apples, place them in the bowl with the lime juice until finished. Place slices onto food dehydrator trays. Dehydrate until dry. Store in sealed glass jars.

Variation: Skip the lime juice, and put apples directly onto dehydrator trays. Great for holiday gifts.

Range and Habitat

Highly cultivated temperate region fruit tree requires warm summers and does best with even moisture and not too much wind. Even though not as common, apple trees can grow in higher elevations and have been known to succeed up to 9,800' in elevation but usually lower. Sun best; partial shade OK.

Comments

Apples can be eaten raw, cooked, or dried. They can also be frozen. Fruit is high in pectin, which is good for making jams.

Apple trees were widely cultivated throughout the period that European immigrants were setting up homesteads in the western United States. Many of these orchards have now been cut down to make way for housing developments. Even so, apple trees can still be found almost everywhere humans have settled.

I found an apple tree in an abandoned field one fall day and was consumed by thoughts about the person, the pioneer, the farmer who struck out to the unsettled west, to the unknown, and planted this tree. I wanted to thank the ancestor who planted this apple tree and tell him how it is doing.

It's very big and old now. Its bark is thickly ridged, and its lower branches droop nearly to the ground. They are dotted prolifically with apples. I like how they grow two together in clusters of four, light reddish and stripped and mottled. The tree is so tall and gnarled and still, amazingly, fertile. Apples absolutely cover its crown, well above where I stood on the ground. I walked inside its giant sweeping arms, and no one on the sidewalk could see me. I could pick your tree's apples in the privacy of its embrace. The bugs were sharing some of the apples, but not too many, except where they blanketed the ground. I ate one while it was still attached to the branch and thought about who you might have been. I know you were thoughtful and took care about what kind of apple tree you planted, because these apples were the sweetest. I know you thought about it, about how to feed your family. I wanted you to know that you are feeding the future. And the future is grateful.

Recipes

An entire cookbook could be written about apples, but I'll narrow it down to just a couple of recipes.

RECIPE

Frozen Apples

To freeze, slice apples and remove the cores. Spread slices out on cookie sheets and place in the freezer. After several hours, when slices of apples are frozen, remove from cookie sheet and place in large Tupperware containers. Store sealed in freezer. Use throughout the winter to make pie, apple crisp, muffins, or smoothies.

RECIPE

Baked Apples

Preheat oven to 350°F. Remove cores from several large apples. Spray a glass baking pan with coconut oil. Place apples in pan. Into the holes left when you removed the cores, add honey, walnuts, fresh-ground cinnamon, and fresh-ground nutmeg. Cook until apples are collapsing and honey mixture is bubbling. Serve warm.

Variation: Serve with vanilla ice cream.

BLUE SPRUCE
Picea pungens

Family: Pinaceae

Other names: Colorado blue spruce, silver spruce, *pino real*, *Picea parryana*, *Picea commutata*

Description

This stately, almost iridescent native conifer (cone-producing evergreen tree) reaches 70'–115' in height. Stiff, stout, prickly needles are often noticeably and dramatically blue hued. The color can range from green or turquoise to powdery or iridescent blue. New needles can be from powder blue to greenish.

Needles are four-sided and about ½"–1¼" long with white stripes. Cones are long, narrow cylinders about 2½"–4½" long, light brown and papery, and notable by the wavy teeth along the scale tips. Shake hands with blue spruce and it will bite. Seed production begins after twenty years.

Range and Habitat
Idaho, Wyoming, and the Four Corners states; very limited in Montana. A reasonably common mountainous species; found on high slopes, in mixed forests,

RECIPE

Richie's Blue Spruce Beer

This is only very mildly alcoholic, similar to kombucha. Feel free to experiment by adding different amounts of ingredients to change it up. To make blue spruce beer, you will need the following:

1 large cooking kettle (8 quart or larger)
Several 1- to 2-liter glass bottles with tightly fitting lids, such as beer growlers or 40-ounce beer bottles (2-liter soda bottles can also be used), cleaned and sanitized with sanitizing solution
Funnel
1¼ gallons fresh water
3–6 ounces fresh blue spruce tips, including needles and stems (Fresh-growth tips in springtime work great, but anytime of year is OK.)
½–¾ ounce dried hops or 1–2 ounces fresh hops
1 small to medium-size piece of ginger root, bruised and cut into chunks
2–3 cups sugar or molasses, depending on desired sweetness
1 package baker's yeast

Bring the water to a boil; add the spruce tips, hops, and ginger. Continue with a light boil for 40 minutes, with a lid partly covering the kettle.

Remove from heat, and pour the mixture through a strainer into another container. Add the sugar or molasses, and stir until completely dissolved and mixed. Allow the mixture to cool until the pot is just warm to the touch.

Add the yeast, and stir vigorously for a couple minutes. Cover pot with good-fitting lid; let sit for 24–48 hours.

Using the funnel, pour the mixture into the bottles. Fill each container halfway at first. Shake it around to aerate the mixture, then fill the bottle completely, leaving about 1" of headspace. Secure the lid tightly, and let the bottles sit for about 5 days at room temperature (around 70°F).

and along streambanks from about 6,700'–11,500' in elevation. Does not grow all the way up to tree line. Prefers moister areas. Often found in Douglas fir and Engelmann spruce forests and along waterways, often with cottonwoods.

Comments

The inner bark is nutritious and can be dried, ground, and mixed into other foods. It is not recommended to harvest bark from the trunk of a tree, as this can severely compromise the tree's ability to bring nutrients to the branches and can result in the tree's death. Instead harvest inner bark from small side branches.

Tea can be made from the fresh needles, which can also be chewed to freshen breath. Some sources say that young male catkins can be eaten raw or cooked and that immature female cones, cooked or roasted, are sweet and gooey. The seeds are nutritious and high in fat. Needle beer is also good. Young shoots, stripped of their needles, can be eaten raw.

The tallest blue spruce ever recorded was 126' tall; the oldest was 600 years old. It is the state tree of Colorado and Utah, and is used for shelter by moose, deer, owls, the Jemez Mountain salamander, and the northern goshawk, among others. Blue spruces are also used by bald eagles for breeding.

PIÑON PINE
Pinus edulis

Family: Pinaceae
Other names: Colorado pinyon, 2-needled piñon, pinyon pine, Rocky Mountain pinyon pine

Description

This relatively small, compact, bushy native evergreen tree often has a crooked trunk and spreading crown. It grows 15'–45' tall. Needles are green, less than 1" to about 4⅓" long and remain on the tree for about nine years each. Usually needles are in clusters of two, but sometimes one or three.

Cones are rounded, about 2" long, and somewhat bulbous with very thick

scales. They ripen from green, purplish or reddish to brown. Each female cone produces ten to twenty delectable seeds, two behind each scale. Seed production begins at about twenty-five years of age, and best seed production is at around seventy-five years. Seed production is better in more moist years. Trees produce heavy seeds crops about every three to seven years. Reproduction occurs only by seeds, which are so delicious they are often eaten by wildlife.

A typical tree can live 500 years, some for 1,000 years. A small piñon pine shrub with only a 6"-diameter trunk can be hundreds of years old.

Range and Habitat

Found along the rim of the Grand Canyon and throughout the foothills and deserts of the Four Corners region from about 4,600'–8,900' in elevation. Common in dry areas, piñon-juniper scrublands and regions with hot summers and cold winters.

Comments

I can eat pine nuts like candy. Actually, I would much prefer to eat pine nuts than candy. They are so meaty and sweet and smoky and luscious.

Many of the piñon pines still standing throughout the Southwest are the same trees that provided sustenance to the pre-Columbian people that lived in the Four Corners area—the Navajo, Hopi, Anasazi, and their ancestors—the very same trees. Ponder that with me for a moment, will you. A massive change has happened in the world, and the trees that provided this nutritious delicacy are still standing, not just in pictorials in history books but in real life, right here. It changes the meaning and the romance of history when we realize that old world still exists.

RECIPE

Pine Nut Trail Mix

Pine nuts can be used raw or lightly toasted.

In a bowl combine ½ cup pine nuts and any of the following: fat tender raisins, dried currants, walnuts, dried apples, dried cherries, granola, chocolate chips. Bring on trail hikes for an energizing snack.

Variation: Combine 1 teaspoon honey and 1 tablespoon canola oil, and mix very well. Stir into fruit and nut mixture until mixture is lightly coated with the oil-and-honey mixture. Spread onto a cookie sheet and bake at low heat, 225°F until just browning on the edges. You can also use the food dehydrator. Remove and let cool. Break into pieces, and pack as a trail snack.

In the harsh, dry desert of the southern reaches of the Rocky Mountain range, great and sophisticated societies of well-fed people, of hunters, of medicine specialists, the children of many tribes and descendents of more than 10,000 years on this continent, picked the nuts from these very trees. I can just imagine the great piñon harvests.

This rich, fatty food should be cherished, reserved, eaten in moderation, and appreciated along with the slow, deliberate nature of the great southwestern desert.

PONDEROSA PINE
Pinus ponderosa

Family: Pinaceae

Other names: Big heavy, black jack, bull pine, ponderosa white pine, Sierra brown bark pine, silver pine, western pitch pine, western red pine, western yellow pine, yellow pine, Yosemite pine

WARNING: Some sources warn that needles can harm unborn babies and are reported to be an abortifacient. **Pregnant women should avoid.** Pregnant cows and other mammals will lose their calves if they consume too many pine needles. Large or frequent use of ponderosa pine needles or pitch can cause kidney problems in some people.

Description

Native to the western half of the United States, this large evergreen tree grows 100'–180' tall (sometimes to 250', making it one of the world's tallest pine trees). Its diameter is 2'–6' wide.

The trunk is straight and usually branchless. The trunk is pungently vanilla smelling. The bark is rough and cinnamon or orange-brown colored with black or gray, charred looking markings.

Needles are long, about 5"–11", and usually grouped in threes, though not always. The needle clusters are surrounded at their base by a small papery sheath. Together the needle clusters grow in spacious, rounded tufts. Trees have male and female cones. Female cones are notable by the rigid, thorn-like pricker on the underside of each cone scale. Seeds mature in late summer to fall of the cone's second year.

Range and Habitat

Found from southern British Columbia to New Mexico and throughout the West from sea level to about 9,800' in elevation. Often found in mixed stands with Douglas fir, lodgepole pine, juniper, blue spruce, and quaking aspens, among other species.

Comments

The seeds, inner bark (cambium), young male cones, pollen, resin (pitch), and needles (with limitations) are edible.

Collect the inner bark any time, but it is best in spring when the sap is flowing. It is described as tasting like sheep fat. To collect inner bark (of any tree) never take it from the trunk, as this can seriously damage or kill the tree. Harvest from side branches, and think about proper pruning techniques as you do so. If you must harvest from the trunk, do **not** ring (girdle) the tree

---

RECIPE

Ponderosa Needle Tea

Harvest a half-handful or so of needles. Place in tea steeper with 2 sprigs mint, 5 rose hips, and 10 squawbush berries. Pour boiling water directly over tea mixture. Allow to steep for 5 to 20 minutes. Add honey; stir and enjoy.

NOTE: This makes an excellent holiday gift for friends and relatives. Place ingredients together in a decorative jar.

CAUTION: Do not use during pregnancy.

Fried Cambium

Harvest inner bark by stabbing tree with sharp knife. Cut a small square from tree. Remove outer bark, and shave off strips of cambium layer. It will be white or cream colored. Cut into thin strips like french fries. Fry in hot vegetable oil and top with sea salt.

unless your intention is to kill the tree (forest thinning for forest health or fire mitigation purposes).

Take a strip that is about one-tenth the circumference of the trunk or, for a large tree, the size of your hand. Scrape the cambium from the outer bark. It can be eaten raw, roasted, boiled, fried, or dried and pounded into flour and used in baking or stews.

Young male cones can be eaten cooked. Harvest before they open, and boil. Small oil-rich seeds can be harvested from female cones in late summer or fall of the cone's second year. They can be eaten raw or cooked.

Needles are used medicinally in tea for colds, coughs, fevers, and other medicinal purposes. **Not for pregnant women.** Warmed pitch can be used to help remove splinters.

DOUGLAS FIR
Pseudotsuga menziesii

Family: Pinaceae
Other names: Rocky Mountain Douglas fir, Douglas spruce, Oregon pine
Lookalikes: All evergreen conifers

Description

This fragrant native conifer (evergreen) tree is not a true fir (*Abies* genus). In the Rocky Mountains it grows to about 100' high. The trunk reaches about 3' in diameter.

Notable by the three-pronged bracts that extend from beneath the scales of the cones. The story goes that in order to escape a forest fire, lots of frightened mice scampered over to the Douglas fir trees and took shelter under the shingles of their cones. When you look at the cones with a bit of imagination, you can still see the little feet and butts of the mice sticking out.

Cones are light brown and 2"–4" long. They hang from the branches and are readily visible both on the tree and on the ground below. (Compare to true firs, which have cones only toward the very top of the trees,

FORAGER NOTE: Look for the mouse feet and tail sticking out of the cone.

and they disintegrate before falling to the ground.)

The needles are flat, not sharp and prickly, and have white lines on the underside. They are dark green, bluish, or yellow-green and ¾"–1¼" long. Bark changes with age.

Range and Habitat

Coastal and mountainous tree found from British Columbia and Alberta to New Mexico from sea level to 11,000' in elevation. Common in montane and subalpine zones and forested hills.

Douglas fir is a very common tree in the Rocky Mountain region. It also grows in coastal areas, where it is much larger and reaches 80'–200' or more in height and 15' across.

Comments

Inner bark can be eaten. It is best to harvest inner bark from smaller branches rather than the trunk. Harvesting from the trunk can kill or severely compromise the health of the tree, especially if not done properly. If harvesting from the trunk, take only a small portion, about the size of your hand, and never girdle the tree (i.e., do not take a strip that goes all the way around the trunk).

RECIPE

Marrow and Ground Cones

Grind cones well in food processor or blender until powdered.

Combine 1 cup powdered Douglas fir cones in saucepan with 2 cups bone marrow. Cook over low-medium heat until combined and marrow has liquefied. Cook at a very low simmer for a few more minutes. Allow to cool.

Serve in small spoonful as a garnish. This delicacy goes well atop dried bite-size pieces of summer squash or fresh crusty bread.

As with all conifers, I enjoy chewing on the raw needles. They are soft and delicious. Use as a breath freshener or in place of chewing gum or mints. They also make a great tea and can be used to make a simple syrup for flavoring drinks and desserts.

Douglas fir is the second tallest tree in the United States, having been recorded up to 329' tall. (Only the redwood is taller.)

Honeybees

HONEYBEES
Apis mellifera

Family: Apidae

Other names: European honeybee, western honeybee

WARNING: Honeybees do sting, although much less often than wasps. Honeybees are usually very docile when encountered away from the hive and will not sting unless threatened. However, they will sting if one gets too close to a hive or tries to get to the honey. A sting from one bee is usually not too bad, but stings by many bees can be quite painful. Some people are **deathly allergic** to bee stings.

Pay very close attention to what happens after you or someone else is stung. Most people will get a small welt, and pain will subside after several minutes. If a person is allergic to bee stings, the reaction can be much worse, even deadly. If the welt grows; hives appear anywhere on the body; the eyes, throat, face, or any part of the body begin to swell; or the person has trouble breathing or asthma-like symptoms develop, **seek medical attention immediately.** Anaphylaxis and death can result.

Description

Honeybees have three main body parts—head, thorax, and abdomen—and are about ½" long. Honeybees typically have alternating orange-yellow and black stripes. Honeybee midsections are rounded, not constricted like those of wasps. They are densely hairy, less so on the abdomen.

Generally there are three different types of bees within a colony. The females consist of the worker bees and usually one active queen. The drones are the males. The queen is noticeably larger than the others and typically can be distinguished by her larger size and lack of stripes. The queen's sole purpose is to lay eggs and be fed and cared for

by the worker bees. The drones' only purpose is to mate with the queen.

Worker bees do most of the work in the colony, including cleaning the hive; feeding and cleaning larvae; tending to the queen; guarding and patrolling the hive; heating or cooling the hive; and foraging for pollen, nectar, honeydew, water, and tree sap. It is from the collection of these things that the bees produce honey. Honey is produced to feed the colony and to get the colony through the winter, when the entire colony hibernates in the hive.

Comments

In addition to the potential for getting stung, wild honey collecting is **not advised** due to the massive decline in honeybee populations around the world. At this time in history, it is essential that we all take the utmost care to protect the bee populations. Given the extreme importance of honeybees to the pollination of flowering plants and the stress they are under due to widespread pesticide use, genetically modified organism (GMO) monocropping, habitat destruction, and harmful industrial beekeeping practices, bees in the wild should be revered and left to continue their natural life cycle. Taking their honey places unnecessary stress on them. Unless you are extremely knowledgeable about appropriate gathering techniques, **do not harvest wild honey.**

Honeybees are one of nature's most remarkable creations, both because they produce delicious honey and because they have a very complex social order.

There are many other types of bees, ranging from a tiny bee barely millimeters long to a very large bee that can be 1½" long. There are also many species of wasps that have similar features as bees. But only the honeybee of the genus *Apis,* of which there are eight species, actually produces honey.

RECIPE

Hot Honey Sundae

Perfect to share in one big bowl with your honey. Choose your favorite version of vanilla ice cream (organic cow's milk ice cream; icy sorbet; or a vegan, nondairy, frozen pureed tofu with vanilla and brown sugar). In a small saucepan over very low heat, heat some honey until just warm. Spoon honey on top of two scoops of ice cream. Top generously with crushed peanuts.

INDEX

ABOUT THE AUTHOR

Liz Brown Morgan is the founder of Backyard Agrarian and the inventor of TareWare. She is also a yoga teacher and a sustainability activist and writer. She has been a wilderness guide, a whitewater raft guide, a professional gardener, and an environmental lawyer. Liz holds a BA in native American studies, an MA in environmental law and policy, and a JD. Learn more or contact her at www.BackyardAgrarian.com.